SEX IN THE SONG OF SONGS

MARK & GRACE
DRISCOLL

Real Romance: Sex in the Song of Songs
Copyright © 2023 by Mark & Grace Driscoll

For information, contact XO Marriage™
P.O Box 59888
Dallas, Texas 75229
1-800-380-6330
xomarriage.com

XO Publishing

ISBN: 978-1-950113-93-4 (Paperback)
ISBN: 978-1-950113-94-1 (eBook)
ISBN: 978-1-950113-95-8 (Audiobook)

23 24 25 26 27—5 4 3 2 1

Contents

Preface

WHAT SCRIPTURE REALLY SAYS ABOUT SEX

God used the Bible to save our marriage.

We met when we were 17 and in high school. We had both been in unhealthy dating relationships previously that were sexual and sinful. When we met, we had little to no clue about how to have a healthy romantic relationship. So we did what most people do—we rushed into a deep, emotional connection too quickly, started sleeping together, and did not seek wise counsel or anything that would resemble godly help. We cared for one another but were clueless about how to take care of one another.

I (Mark) was a non-Christian; raised a Catholic, but I had no personal relationship with God. The only Bible I can remember was our giant family Bible that sat on the coffee table in our living room covered in enough dust to write "fornication" on it with your finger. Grace was a pastor's daughter who knew the Lord but was in a prodigal daughter season and was not walking with Him (which explains why she was walking with me). As we headed off to different universities, we were headed for the same misery. Thankfully, the Lord not only saved us from going to hell, but He also saved us from ourselves and from making hell of our lives.

The Bible Saved Our Marriage

I (Grace) had enough conviction left to know God's plan for me was *not* to be dating a non-Christian. I should have broken up with Mark, but instead I bought him a Bible as a gift. I wasn't spending much time reading my own Bible, but hypocritically, I thought *he* needed one. I knew the Bible would tell us what we should do. Despite my lack of wisdom, God showed incredible grace to Mark and me. We feel very humbled to be able to teach what we learned the hard way so that others don't have to go through the same experience. The Bible has been a foundational part of anything good in our marriage. We are excited to help you learn from a book of the Bible, as we study Song of Songs.

I (Mark) became a Christian reading the Bible that Grace gave me. I quickly found a wonderful, Bible-teaching church and became excited about learning from God's Word, which has led me to preach through books of the Bible as a senior pastor since 1996. Today, we are both teaching the Bible most weeks to the men and women at Trinity Church, which we founded as a family ministry in Scottsdale, Arizona, along with our five children (the two oldest of whom are now married). We give our Bible teaching away to help people in their relationships with God and others through RealFaith Ministries.

Without the Bible, we would not be married. Either we would have so badly ruined our romantic relationship while dating that we would never have made it to marriage, or if we did marry, it would have ended badly. We have sought to build our life, marriage, family, ministry, and legacy on the Bible, and God's Word has never failed us. We want to be honest with you so that you can be honest with God and each other. If God can take a lost guy who was sleeping with a pastor's daughter and give us a good marriage and a godly family along with a Bible teaching ministry, then there is certainly hope for you!

The most popular Bible book we have ever taught—and the one that got us into the most trouble—is the Song of Songs, which is also called the Song of Solomon. We started by teaching it in small groups to couples, then larger classes, and eventually large conferences around the nation. Out of this teaching came our most popular and *controversial* sermon series ever.

In *Real Romance*, our goal is to help you build your marriage on the Song of Songs. It is the only book of the Bible devoted exclusively to marriage. If you have made mistakes, committed sins, and done things wrong in your life and relationship, we can relate. We got our personal and sexual relationship wrong before God made it right by renewing our minds and reworking our desires by His Spirit through His Word. The reason we are calling this Bible study project *Real Romance* is simple: we will be real with you about our faults, flaws, and failures as well as about how God's hope, help, and healing have allowed us to work through the pain and get to the pleasure of now 30 years of faithful Christian marriage. We love you, we are excited for you, and we know that the same God who has blessed us will bless you if you live under the authority of His Word. Why? Because God does not just bless people—He also blesses people who place themselves under His Word. Thank you for the great honor of allowing us to be on this double date as, together, we enjoy real romance by studying the Song of Songs. We will start by looking at sex in the Scripture generally, then sex in the Song of Songs specifically.

Sex in Scripture

In the days of the Old Testament, when the poetic Hebrew love story of the Song of Songs was written, God's people were surrounded and seduced by all sorts of sexual sin, much like we face today. There were fertility cults in which business, spirituality, and sex were integrated into one demonic, worldly system, not unlike the porn and adult entertainment industry of our day.

The Canaanite demon gods were believed to be naked sexual beings who were to be worshipped through sex and erotic, pornographic poetry. Their vile blend of debased sexuality and demonic spirituality included large Ashtoreth poles. These were male phallic symbols used as advertisements to draw people from miles around to enjoy sex without boundaries as part of worship. It was common for ancient worship to include temples that were the equivalent of a brothel and strip club, complete with male and female prostitutes. Other world religions such as Hinduism historically have also had prostitutes as part of their demonic worship and sensual discipleship guides like the Kama Sutra.

In the days of the New Testament, things were not any better. Greek culture, which predominated the Roman Empire, encouraged older men to groom young boys for sex. The cities in which Christianity spread were filled with perverted sexuality married to demonic spirituality. This included temples in cities like Corinth where the demonic fertility goddess Aphrodite had over a thousand male and female prostitutes waiting to have sex without limits. This explains why Paul's letter to the Corinthians instructs Christians not to have sex with a close relative or a person of the same sex, engage in orgies, fornicate by living and sleeping together before marriage, commit adulterous sex outside of marriage, abandon their God-given sex and gender by cross-dressing, or return to having sex at the pagan temples. These new Christians in Paul's day were exposed to the same kind of gender spectrum tolerance and diversity sex education in the name of pride that inundates people in our own day. The demons at work in the past continue their work in the present. Thankfully, the Bible is not old but timeless and, therefore, always timely.

A wealth of scientific research has established the brain as our most important sex organ. In the developing field of brain science, we are learning that our brains not only house our thoughts about sex but also send signals to our bodies that will help or harm our sexual freedom and frequency. For this reason, it is vital for us to begin understanding why God made sex, how God sees sex and guidelines God gives for sex so we can have our minds renewed and our marriages redeemed. Broadly speaking, there are *three ways to view sex: gross, god,* or *gift.*

> "IT IS VITAL FOR US TO BEGIN UNDERSTANDING WHY GOD MADE SEX, HOW GOD SEES SEX AND GUIDELINES GOD GIVES FOR SEX SO WE CAN HAVE OUR MINDS RENEWED AND OUR MARRIAGES REDEEMED."

Sex as Gross

While our bodies and the sexual pleasure they enjoy were custom designed by God, some people sadly see sex as gross or disgusting. This perspective most commonly happens in one of two ways.

One, some bad religious teaching focuses almost entirely on what is sinful and forbidden with little teaching on what the Bible promotes for healthy marital sexuality. At its worst, bad religious teaching presents sex, even within marriage, as a sort of necessary evil for human procreation, or solely to keep the husband from straying out of the marriage and into adultery. This erroneous teaching is often rooted in ancient, non-biblical Greek thought that considered the human body basically evil and the pleasures derived in it as undesirable. Many early Christian teachers were raised with Greek thought and sadly kept some of this faulty mindset long after their conversions. Examples include Tertullian and Ambrose, who preferred human extinction to sex; Origen, who allegorized the Song of Songs and castrated himself; Gregory of Nyssa and Chrysostom, who taught that sex was a result of sin and the fall and not part of God's design; and Jerome, who threw himself into brambles or beat his chest with a rock when sexually tempted and considered too much fun with his wife to be a sin against God. Not only were Catholic priests forbidden to marry, but by the Middle Ages, priests were also encouraged to regulate the frequency, positions, and sensations of married couples so that roughly half the year was filled with days married couples were forbidden from intercourse, which contributed to the Protestant Reformation. The former monk Martin Luther married the nun Katherine. In his teaching, he brought about a complete transformation of marital love and babies as part of a godly life for God's people. The Victorian Age was marked by extreme modesty and a bit of an obsession with eliminating virtually any opportunity for sexuality to be seen publicly. Women were nearly silent in public and covered themselves down to their ankles with long dresses. One debated observation from a traveling British Navy captain in that day was that table and piano legs were even covered to prevent men who saw a naked table leg from being tempted to lustful thoughts. To state the obvious, if a man is sexually aroused by a table leg, then the problem is in his heart and not his furniture.

Two, because of sexual sin they have committed (e.g., fornication, pornography, adultery, etc.), or sexual sin committed against them (e.g., molestation as a child, assault as a teen or adult, rape, adultery, etc.), some people associate the pain of sin with the pleasure of sex and need a renewed mind, as Paul says. These kinds of trauma cause harm to the totality of a person, and if you have had any of these evil experiences, we are deeply sorry for that horrific pain. The best thing you can do is find a godly professional to meet with for wise counsel. There is healing and hope on the other side of abuse, and we want that for you and your marriage.

I (Grace) experienced sexual and emotional abuse in high school that was covered with shame until over 10 years (and five kids) into marriage. The enemy had convinced me I deserved how I had been treated in a relationship before I met Mark, so I didn't consider it "abuse." I was folding laundry when Mark asked a specific question about my past one seemingly normal evening. When I answered about how I was controlled and forced to do things against my will for over two years, I looked over and saw Mark crying (not something that happens regularly). In that moment, we realized

I had experienced abuse in my past and needed healing. I started to understand it had affected our marriage and kept us from the closeness we desired. I won't lie and say the healing process was easy or quick, but I sought Christian trauma counseling and ultimately grew closer to Jesus and Mark in ways I didn't know were possible. I was a victim of abuse, but I had to ultimately take responsibility for some of the decisions I made out of that pain. I'm thankful God brought all of this into the light so I could be free in Him rather than in bondage to the enemy's condemnation. If trauma is part of your story, I want to encourage you that God has healing for you too. The enemy has a plan to destroy you and your marriage, but God has a plan to restore you and bless your marriage. A godly professional filled with the Spirit and the latest insights from trauma therapy could be a great part of your healing journey.

> **THE ENEMY HAS A PLAN TO DESTROY YOU AND YOUR MARRIAGE, BUT GOD HAS A PLAN TO RESTORE YOU AND BLESS YOUR MARRIAGE.**

When both people see sex as gross, the result is what is commonly referred to as a sexless marriage. According to a landmark Pew Survey, a satisfying sexual relationship was the second most important factor of marital satisfaction. No less than 70 percent of adults consider it a "very important" element of marital satisfaction, right behind "faithfulness" which in large part pertains to not straying outside of the marriage for sexual enjoyment.[i] In a study by the Austin Institute for the Study of Family and Culture, 12 percent of all married couples had not had sex for at least three months. Another survey found that within the previous year, 20 percent of couples had not had sex.[ii]

No one knows the exact rate of divorce for sexless marriages, but we can assume it is high since sexual problems in marriage is the third most prevalent reason couples name in divorce surveys. The prevalence of sexless marriages is likely even higher than the statistics indicate. In addition to sexless marriages, there are many marriages that simply have far less sex than would be healthy. Sadly, we have seen this even among pastors and their spouses. We personally know pastors who are in sexless, or less than enough sex, marriages, but they are still preaching and teaching on marriage, conducting premarital and marital counseling, and officiating weddings. It is hard to imagine that their pastoral care of marriages is the best it could be considering their personal lack of healthy marital intimacy. Some years ago, we spoke at a large Valentine's event hosted in a major city by the local Christian radio station. Thousands of people came to hear us teach from the Song of Songs, and in the line where we met people who wanted to say hello, we met multiple young couples from the same well-known conservative local church. These men and women had been married up to a year and had still not consummated their marriage out of fear from bad Christian teaching about sex. Basically, their parents and pastors told them that sex was dirty, nasty, vile, and wrong and to be saved for marriage, which only confused and scared the young couples. Since biblical marriage is being in a covenant that is consummated, it could be argued that they were not even technically married but instead awkward and fearful roommates.

Sex as God

Who or what sets your identity, demands your allegiance, floods your mind, and takes priority in your life is your functional "god." If this is anyone or anything other than the God of the Bible, it is idolatry. What often happens is that we take a good thing, like sex, and make it a "god" thing, thereby making it a bad thing. The result is sexual sin and addiction of any and every sort. This explains why people keep having parades about sexual sin, for which they should be having funerals.

> **WHAT OFTEN HAPPENS IS THAT WE TAKE A GOOD THING, LIKE SEX, AND MAKE IT A "GOD" THING, THEREBY MAKING IT A BAD THING.**

Being married to someone who sees sex as god is difficult because you feel that they don't care as much about your soul, heart, or mind; what matters most to them is your body. This can lead to feeling neglected outside the bedroom and used inside the bedroom. The relationship sadly takes a back seat as the orgasm is almost always in the driver's seat.

When both people see sex as god, the marital relationship is quickly rolling down a steep hill toward the cliff of sexual sin. When both the husband and wife have too liberal sexual boundaries and out-of-order sexual priorities, and they do not help one another avoid temptation, any perversion is possible. The passions of sex are like a fire, and marriage is the hearth that God created to contain it. Whenever it is taken out of the hearth of marriage, sex starts burning down our relationship with God, marriage, family, health, and culture. This explains why there is gender confusion, sexual experimentation, pornography, friends with benefits, sex trafficking, prostitution, strip clubs, robotic sex dolls, sexual addiction, pedophilia, bestiality, fornication, adultery, swinging, sexual assault, and tragically much more.

I (Mark) entered our dating and marriage years seeing sex as god. My parents were clear on healthy sexual boundaries growing up, and I saw enough young girls in my neighborhood get pregnant and be in abusive relationships that I generally stayed out of trouble while I was living at home with my parents. I avoided alcohol and carousing, not out of godly conviction but out of the fear of being trapped in some bad and broken relationship. I believe I would have gotten into a lot of trouble sexually, however, if God had not saved me at the age of 19 early in my freshman year in college. A pivotal life moment came when the fraternity I had recently joined threw its first big, drunken party of the year. I was about to walk into a dark basement room filled with music, girls, and beer when God spoke to me and told me I did not belong there. I was not a Christian, and I was about to walk into a new life that was death. I was startled and unsure what was happening, but I did as I was told and left the party to spend the night sitting in the library alone. The next day the house smelled like beer, and girls awoke hung over and embarrassed. Some were crying as they looked for their shoes and clothes. I moved out of that fraternity right away, and my pledge class ended up getting arrested and spending evenings doing community service and weekends in jail. Like Lot, God literally pulled me out of Sodom and Gomorrah before destruction.

Now, I loved Grace, so I was faithful to her and avoided the typical single years in my 20s, which would have been spent getting in a lot of trouble had God not intervened before I was living on my own. As soon as I started learning what the

Bible taught about sex as a new Christian, I realized I needed to get married young because I knew I would not make it into my early 30s (the age the average guy gets married today) chaste, holy, and healthy. Not knowing about Grace's abuse prior to our meeting, I now see how my view of sex as god put pressure on her in our marriage as she saw sex more as gross. We both needed to heal up and learn a lot to come to a healthy place under the Word of God together.

When one person sees sex as gross and the other sees sex as god, there is a lot of pain, conflict, and lonely frustration felt by both. The person who sees sex as god lives in the despair that their many desires will never be realized in their

> **WHEN ONE PERSON SEES SEX AS GROSS AND THE OTHER SEES SEX AS GOD, THERE IS A LOT OF PAIN, CONFLICT, AND LONELY FRUSTRATION FELT BY BOTH.**

marriage, which can lead to bitterness and wandering outside of the marriage into the sexual sins that consume our culture and constantly pull us toward hell like gravity. The person who sees sex as gross feels inordinate pressure from their spouse, wonders if or when they will commit adultery in some form, and feels devalued and pursued only for sex instead of loved for relationship.

If either of you sees sex as god or gross, you have a very real problem in your marriage. In this case, sex is a broken place that needs healing, which only happens by you both understanding that sex is a gift given from God for you to share with each other to strengthen your marriage.

Sex as Gift

God uniquely and intentionally created our bodies for sex and sexual pleasure. God made us male and female and brought us together for marriage, and our marriage covenant was consummated with the passion and pleasure of sex. God was not shocked that our naked first parents had sex, and He did not send an angel to put a wing between them and shut it down. Sex was His divine will and design—perfect, holy, and before sin and the Fall. God called all this married sexuality "very good" as our first parents were "not ashamed" before sin entered the world. This gift of heterosexual, married sex was given by God for six reasons:

1. Pleasure (Song of Songs)
2. Children (Genesis 1:28)
3. Oneness (Genesis 2:24)
4. Knowledge (Genesis 4:1)
5. Protection (1 Corinthians 7:2–5)
6. Comfort (2 Samuel 12:24).

> **SEX WAS HIS DIVINE WILL AND DESIGN—PERFECT, HOLY, AND BEFORE SIN AND THE FALL.**

It is common for one or both people in a marriage to have an erroneous view of sex that needs to be worked through, healed, and moved on from. This was our case. When we married at the age of 21, I (Mark) was a new Christian who saw sex more as god. I grew up within walking distance of strip clubs, hourly rate motels, and open prostitution on a nearby highway close to a major airport. Thankfully, I didn't participate in any of them, but they were the norm in my neighborhood.

Grace grew up in a Christian home and had abuse that caused her to see sex more as gross. We had a lot of healing and learning to do, and God was gracious to bring us into agreement with the Scriptures that teach sex as a gift from God. What was most helpful to us was learning about sex in the Song of Songs. There, we learned that it's old-school, red-hot monogamy that is seriously sexy.

Sex in the Song of Songs

How does a godly and poor young woman working long hours in the hot sun to help support her single mother and brothers become the wife of a king and one of the most renowned, passionate, and sexually free women the world has ever celebrated?

The answer is found in the biblical book of the Song of Songs, where we meet this glorious peasant princess. She speaks first, is spoken of last, and speaks most frequently throughout this sacred love story. We also meet her friends, brothers, and mother as we see snapshots of her life including childhood, the teen years, engagement, and marriage.

As we study the Song of Songs, our primary focus will be the intimate marital relationship she shares with her husband, Solomon. Through her example, God has much to teach us regarding His plan for sex and marriage. While the Song of Songs is not entirely about sex, the book does contain some especially important lessons on the subject. In fact, this 3,000-year-old collection of love letters is extraordinary in its timeliness.

There are at least three curious facts regarding the Song of Songs. One, depending upon which English translation you read, God is mentioned either zero times or just one time in the entire book.[1] Two, the Song of Songs is never quoted in the New Testament. Three, the Song of Songs never mentions children despite talking a lot about sex, as this book is entirely about the passions and pleasures of marital sex but not the blessing of children.

Before the Greeks, the first philosophers were the Hebrew writers of Old Testament wisdom literature. Job probes suffering and evil, Ecclesiastes explores the meaning of life, and Song of Songs plumbs the depths of love, sex, and marriage in a poetic way that is neither clinical nor crass. It does not read like an awkward high school health class depiction of sex or the inappropriate version more common in the locker room. Interestingly, Jewish tradition is to read the Song of Songs every year on Shabbat during Passover.[iii]

> ## SONG OF SONGS PLUMBS THE DEPTHS OF LOVE, SEX, AND MARRIAGE IN A POETIC WAY THAT IS NEITHER CLINICAL NOR CRASS.

In every age, especially our own, people devote an extraordinary amount of time, money, and energy in pursuit of sex, making it the most popular counterfeit religion in the world. In Romans 1:24–25, the apostle Paul says people either worship God their Creator and enjoy His creation—including our bodies—or they worship creation as God and, in sexual sin, offer their bodies as living sacrifices (which is the definition of worship in Romans 12:1). Paul goes on to explain that those who worship creation invariably worship the human body,

---

1 8:6

because it is the apex of God's creation. Nothing in creation is as beautiful, wonderful, and enjoyable as the human body. In this upending of rightful worship, sex becomes a false religion and the sex act a perverse sacrament.

In sum, the greatest threat to Christianity is sex. Everyone who settles for the worship of sex as a god is truly seeking an intimacy, joy, and connection that can only be found through faith and relationship with the real God. As G. K. Chesterton said, "Every man who knocks on the door of a brothel is looking for God." Today, sex is a religion, and the various gender and sexual interest groups are denominations in that religion. Like traditional churches, cults, and religions, the religion of sex is now moving into children's ministry, seeking to disciple kids everywhere from the classroom to entertainment and social media. Perhaps no time in Western history has been as needy for solid Bible teaching on sex, gender, marriage, and sexuality.

In Scripture, we see that God is our Creator. He created us not on a gender spectrum of our choosing but rather in binary and fixed male and female categories chosen by Him. Our male and female bodies were created for pleasure and marital oneness.[2] God's original intent was chastity and fidelity in heterosexual marriage; we worship God in part by obeying Him in pure pleasure. A fictitious demon in *The Screwtape Letters* by C. S. Lewis admits the origins of sex: "Never forget that when we are dealing with any pleasure in its healthy and normal and satisfying form, we are, in a sense, on the Enemy's [God's] ground. I know we have won many a soul through pleasure. All the same, it is His invention, not ours. He made the pleasures."[iv]

Through the story of the Song of Songs, we learn how to have sex that is free—free from sin, idolatry, guilt, shame, condemnation, death, and separation from God—by having free

---

2 See Genesis 1–2.

and frequent marital intimacy. We will study the Song of Songs to learn how to worship God the Creator, enjoy His creation, and not worship His creation (our bodies and their pleasures) as a false god.

Christians throughout history have struggled to determine how to have a healthy and balanced sexuality. Some people have chosen to essentially kill their sexual desires out of a fear of temptation to sin. Other people lead destructive lives of secret sin that are eventually exposed, causing much pain. Still others are simply confused, uncertain of how to speak to their spouse and children about sex, unsure of what is compatible and incompatible with the teaching of Scripture.

Our study of the Song of Songs is meant neither to kill our desires nor permit them to drive us into deadly sin. We will invite the Holy Spirit to cultivate our desires and drive them toward our spouse according to the wisdom God gives us in His Word. We will learn about gender, dating, marriage, and sex as God intends. This Bible study will have insight for young and old, parents and grandparents, singles and engaged, and of course, husbands and wives. As the book title suggests, the Song of Songs is perhaps the greatest lyric ever composed—a warm dialogue between two lovers, a conversation of the heart that crescendos into a beautiful duet. This poetic exchange reflects the very heart of our Trinitarian God from whom love, intimacy, and musical expression flow.

Song of Songs is rather shocking, especially when we consider it was written 3,000 years ago to a highly religious, very conservative Eastern culture. While it is frank, it is not crass, which serves as a good distinction for God's people. People who are a bit more conservative than God, and therefore religious when it comes to sex, have tended to try avoiding or explaining the book away. In the world of ancient Judaism, you were not supposed to read the book until you were 30 years of age or married.[v] Throughout history, some Bible interpreters have tried to encourage the book to be written metaphorically as poetic imagery about our relationship with God. To be sure, we are to have a loving relationship with God, but the Song of Songs is firstly about the passions and pleasures of married love life.

The book is far freer and franker than many Christian scholars who have tried to teach it. Not used to blushing while teaching the Bible, it has been common to overlook the obvious and straightforward literal meaning of the poetic book—that God delights in husbands and wives who enjoy the sexual freedom He gives them within the limits of Scripture. To interpret the Song of Songs otherwise results in some of the strangest Bible teaching in the history of the Christian church. Jewish Bible

> **GOD DELIGHTS IN HUSBANDS AND WIVES WHO ENJOY THE SEXUAL FREEDOM HE GIVES THEM WITHIN THE LIMITS OF SCRIPTURE.**

scholars have generally interpreted it as an allegory about the loving relationship between God and the nation of Israel, with Christian scholars saying it is primarily about Jesus Christ and His loving relationship with His bride, the Church. There may be some lessons to learn from this, or any other healthy marriage, about the Christian life, but that is not the main point.

Origen (185–253) is the heavyweight champion of interpreting the Song of Songs allegorically instead of literally. In addition to preaching a series of sermons on the book, he also published a 10-volume commentary using such liberty and creativity with connecting every concept to something spiritual and nothing physical so that in the end an entire book of the Bible is as clear as mud. In an effort to remove any sense of "carnal lust" from the book, Bernard of Clairvaux (1009–1153) preached 86 sermons on just the first two chapters of the Song of Songs, trying to remove anything that was remotely sexual in his interpretation. Others following in this wake of being more conservative than God include church father Augustine, Methodist John Wesley, Puritan Matthew Henry, and many others. In case you were uncertain, 80 concubines (6:8) are not the 80 heresies prophesied to attack the church. Also, the two breasts (4:5; 7:8) are not the Old and New Testaments that provide us the milk of God's Word. These kinds of interpretations reveal more about what is wrong with the scholars than what is written in the Scriptures.

Throughout our study together of this ancient Hebrew love song, you will notice three primary characters in the poetic story. One, the wife, speaks first and most. Contrary to some religious stereotypes, she is a passionate, strong, and vocal woman who may have been the young Abishag who cared for Solomon's dying father, David, as she fits the profile of a poor working-class woman from the same region of Shulammite (6:13). One Bible dictionary says that Shulammite is the "Name or title of Solomon's lover in his Song (Sg 6:13). Her identity is not certain. Some suggest that Shulammite refers to a woman from the city of Shunem. Her designation as Shunammite was perhaps changed to Shulammite for its similarity in sound to Solomon's Hebrew name. Shunem was situated in the land of Issachar near Mt. Gilboa (1 Samuel 28:4). It was from this city that Abishag, the beautiful Shunammite woman, was called to nurse King David in his later years (1 Kgs 1:1–4, 15; 2:17–22). It is possible that Abishag became the beloved Shulammite maiden of Solomon's song."[vi]

Another Bible Dictionary describes "Abishag the Shu-namite" as "A beautiful woman from Shunem who became David's nurse in the last days of his life. After David's death, Adonijah wanted to marry Abishag. He persuaded Bathsheba to advocate for him before the king. Solomon suspected this request to be an aspiration for the throne and put Adonijah to death (1 Kgs 2:17–25)."[vii]

Although we cannot be entirely sure about who Solomon's wonderful wife is in the Song of Songs, Abishag is the most likely candidate. To keep things simple, we will refer to her by the more western version of her name—"Abbi"—most of the time.

Two, the husband, is Solomon, who is named six times[3] and referred to as "the king" three times.[4] He was the product of adultery between Bathsheba and David, who planned the murder of her first husband. Despite having great wisdom and the fact that he should have learned about the evils of sexual sin from his parents, Solomon nonetheless fell into great sin with 700 wives and 300 concubines—something we will study in more detail later in this book.

Third, their friends speak throughout the book, giving wise counsel and support for their relationship. God often speaks and works through people who are filled with the Spirit to help us see and walk in His will for our life and marriage. Healthy, godly, and confidential people are hard to find, but having a few of these people in your life is a tremendous blessing.

Lastly, as we study Song of Songs together, there is one inter-pretive issue to note. Some commentators see the book as writ-ten in chronological order. It starts with free and frank discus-sions as the couple moves toward marriage, including abstaining from sexual activity until they are wed. Next, the book focuses

3 1:5; 3:7, 9, 11; 8:11–12

4 1:4, 12; 7:6

on the ups and downs of married life and concludes with a chapter devoted to looking back at each partner's upbringing and family of origin, all of which helped shaped them as adults. I (Mark) tend to lean toward this chronological view.

Other commentators view the book more like a photo album with various thematic snapshots throughout their life together as a couple. There are pictures from their dating life and their married years, but not necessarily in chronological order. This view is largely driven by the very frank and personal discussions early in the book. If the book is written in chronological order, then the intimate discussions early on could cause the awakening of sexual discussion before they should happen, which would violate one of the recurring themes of the book. Grace tends toward this interpretive approach.

Either way, the Song of Songs is filled with helpful healing and wisdom for your sex life and marriage. We like to say that there are closed-handed and open-handed issues in Christianity. The closed-handed issues are primary matters that are essential to knowing Jesus Christ as your Lord and Savior and living according to the Word of God by the power of the Holy Spirit. The open-handed issues are secondary matters that are important but less so than primary matters. We agree on the essential and primary open-handed issues, and even after decades of marriage and ministry teaching the Bible, we still have some open-handed secondary issues we disagree on that we discuss but would never divide over because our marriage matters more than our differences. We encourage you to pursue this same unity and diversity in your own marriage and are honored that you would welcome us to help your marriage flourish. With that said, we have elected to make the study of Song of Songs in this book based on themes rather than taking the chronological approach. Regardless of the approach you personally take, the principles for your marriage are the same with either interpretive view.

The odds are high that after reading this section there are some things in your past or present that you are feeling some conviction about. Don't let that condemn you or cause you to stop pressing forward in your healing and learning. The fact that God is allowing us to help you learn about sex from the Bible shows His gracious irony. As a new Christian, I (Mark) heard a talk at my first church about something called "fornication" that was for us college students. I had never really heard about fornication, but from what the pastor said it seemed obvious that Grace and I were fornicating. So I called the pastor and told him I had a friend who I feared was fornicating (though I declined to tell him it was Grace). I tried everything I could to find a way to get him to say that the Bible did have some sort of loophole for a dating couple to be sleeping together, and he was adamant that there wasn't one. So I did what I think was my first topical Bible study, trying my best to find a loophole that would allow fornication in God's eyes. I could not find a loophole, so I called Grace to tell her we had been fornicating. She informed me that she *already* knew because she grew up in church. So we stopped fornicating. The point is this: if God can take our story and patiently and graciously renew our minds and restore our relationship by the Holy Spirit working through the Bible, there is every hope that He can and will do the same for you.

To prepare for the next chapter and the rest of this Bible study, please set aside some time with your phones off to hold hands, pray for one another, look each other in the eye, and have a respectful and loving conversation initiated by the following questions. We love you and are praying for you as you start this first step of your journey toward a more sacred romance!

" IF GOD CAN TAKE OUR STORY AND PATIENTLY AND GRACIOUSLY RENEW OUR MINDS AND RESTORE OUR RELATIONSHIP BY THE HOLY SPIRIT WORKING THROUGH THE BIBLE, THERE IS EVERY HOPE THAT HE CAN AND WILL DO THE SAME FOR YOU. "

FACE-TO-FACE QUESTIONS
for Couple Discussion

1. When you first met, did you see sex more as gross, god, or gift?

2. Today, do you see sex more as gross, god, or gift?

3. What experiences and teachings were most helpful and unhelpful in your view of sex?

4. What are some of your favorite sexual memories with your spouse?

5. As you read the chapter, did the Holy Spirit convict you of anything you need to apologize to your spouse about regarding your view of sex and how it has affected your marriage relationship?

6. What are you hoping God does in your marriage relationship as you study the Song of Songs together?

7. How can you pray for one another as you study the Song of Songs together?

Chapter 1

LET HIM KISS ME
1:1–7

1:1 Solomon's Song of Songs.

She

> **2** Let him kiss me with the kisses of his mouth—
> for your love is more delightful than wine.
> **3** Pleasing is the fragrance of your perfumes;
> your name is like perfume poured out.
> No wonder the young women love you!
> **4** Take me away with you—let us hurry!
> Let the king bring me into his chambers.

Friends

> We rejoice and delight in you;
> we will praise your love more than wine.

She

> How right they are to adore you!
> **5** Dark am I, yet lovely,
> daughters of Jerusalem,
> dark like the tents of Kedar,

1

like the tent curtains of Solomon.
6 Do not stare at me because I am dark,
because I am darkened by the sun.
My mother's sons were angry with me
and made me take care of the vineyards;
my own vineyard I had to neglect.
7 Tell me, you whom I love,
where you graze your flock
and where you rest your sheep at midday.
Why should I be like a veiled woman
beside the flocks of your friends?

———————

In every romantic relationship, there comes a time when it transitions from a friendship, where you are getting to know one another, to the butterflies in your stomach, can't stop thinking about one another phase, and the eventual walk down the aisle to do the kind of stuff Marvin Gaye sings about.

When did this pivot from friendship to romantic relationship happen for you and your beloved? As we settle into our marriage and years or even decades pass, it's good to remind ourselves of how and why we fell in love. What was this like for you? For your beloved?

> **IT'S GOOD TO REMIND OURSELVES OF HOW AND WHY WE FELL IN LOVE.**

Grace and I met at the age of 17 at a large public high school. Although she was only five weeks older than me, she was a senior when I (Mark) was a junior. Her lifelong friend sat in front of me in a class, told me all about Grace, and introduced us. I knew about Grace but did not really get to know her until we had our first phone call and went out on our first date. Driving in my first car (a 1956 Chevy), I was so nervous to meet her pastor father and mother that I drove around their block a few times, mustering up the courage to face whatever awkwardness was required to spend time with her. Within a couple of weeks or months of spending time together, I knew that she was my dream girl. So I bought her a jewelry box as a gift and told her my plan was to put an engagement ring in it one day. Grace has been the girl I cannot live without since the day we met, and after Jesus Christ she is the greatest blessing in my life. If she were not in my life, everything would be different, and nothing would be better.

Mark was popular in high school, but I (Grace) was shy. When I heard he wanted to talk to me, I couldn't believe it. I was nervous, but he had a reputation of being nice to girls and protective, so I was interested in what that was like after being in a harmful relationship. He called me, and we talked very naturally for three hours on a phone that had a cord (back in the 80s)! From there we spent our dates getting to know each other, laughing, and building a friendship. I didn't believe him when he told me "I was the one," because I thought he was too good for me, but it all eventually came together as God planned.

The Genesis of Marriage

The first marriage in history is how the Bible begins in the opening chapters of Genesis. God made the world "good" but said one thing was "not good"—that man was alone. So God made woman and brought her to the man like a father walking his daughter down the aisle and like the pastor officiating the first marriage. Adam sang a poetic love song to his bride as the first words we have recorded from any human being in history. Adam and Eve then consummated their marriage, and they were naked without shame and "one flesh" (see Genesis 2:24). Since there were only two people alive, both Adam and Eve saw their spouse as their standard of beauty, and their sex life was a beautiful and godly part of their marriage covenant. This principle cannot be overstated in the midst of a pornified planet: we do not have a standard of beauty to which we compare our spouses, because God gifted them to us as *our* standard of beauty!

Admittedly, this means our standard of beauty changes as our spouse changes. If your marriage begins with a husband who has a full head of hair and six pack abs, but some decades later his bangs have gone home to be with the Lord and he now has cooler abs, then you need to adjust your mindset. It is helpful to try and look your best as you age for your spouse, but in the end, gravity remains undefeated, and we must give our spouse some grace just as we hope for some ourselves.

Marriage and sex started really wonderful but have become really awful. Since sin entered the world, pain, problems, and perils have invaded sex and marriage. The good news is that God can and does heal, restore, and bless people who live under the authority of His Word. We like to say that many couples need a new marriage, but they don't need a new spouse.

God can give you a *new* marriage with the *same* spouse! When both the husband and wife are filled with the Spirit and living in obedience to God's Word, they have a guaranteed success rate in marriage. This brings us to the Song of Songs, the most frank and passionate book in the Bible about sex and marriage.

> **WE LIKE TO SAY THAT MANY COUPLES NEED A NEW MARRIAGE, BUT THEY DON'T NEED A NEW SPOUSE.**

The Song of Songs is part of an enormous body of work from Solomon that includes 3,005 proverbs and 1,005 songs. In calling it the *Song of Songs*, the point is that these are his greatest songs, much like calling Jesus Christ "King of kings" and "Lord of lords" points to His preeminence. In this chapter, we will study the first sensual song between the man and his beloved. We begin by seeing a female who is very free.

Covenant vs. Contract

The days leading up to marriage can be incredible times for learning and growing. This was our case. Between our junior and senior years of college, we were married in our hometown, which was hundreds of miles away from college. The night before our wedding, I (Mark) needed a place to sleep before we headed from our honeymoon to the rental house at our college. Grace's great-uncle John kindly invited me to spend the night at his condo. Uncle John and his wife, Aunt Gladys, did not have any children, and they loved Grace and treated her like a granddaughter. Aunt Gladys had Alzheimer's, so

Uncle John placed her in a care facility for her own safety, as she was continually wandering and becoming lost. Uncle John remained devoted to his wife, visiting her multiple times every day even though she tragically did not remember him anymore. At every visit she would ask him who he was, and he would patiently and kindly remind her that he was her husband and had devoted his entire adult life to her.

The night before our wedding, Uncle John sat down with me in his home to make sure that I was fully devoted to Grace. He asked me if I would love her and be faithful to her, even if she forgot who I was. Uncle John was asking me to have a covenant marriage with Grace and not a contract. The Bible speaks of marriage in terms of a covenant,[5] and it speaks of covenant relationships hundreds of times with numerous words. The heart of covenant is lovingkindness— the consistent, ever-faithful, relentless, constantly pursuing, lavish, extravagant, unrestrained, one-way love of God. Various English Bible translations use words such as love, lovingkindness, mercy, steadfast love, loyal love, devotion, commitment, and reliability to translate the concept of covenant into English. When our children were little, we would often read to them from the Jesus Storybook Bible, which calls covenant love the "Never Stopping, Never Giving Up, Unbreaking, Always & Forever Love."[viii]

For Christians, our relationship with our spouse is supposed to follow the grace-based covenantal relationship God has with His people, whom He refers to as a beloved bride.

> Marriage is a principal image in the Scriptures for describing the binding covenantal relationship between YHWH and

---

5 Proverbs 2:17; Malachi 2:14

Israel[6] and again between Christ and the church.[7] The fore-most idea conveyed through this image is not sexual union but complete steadfastness, fidelity, and loyalty.[ix]

Some Christian traditions consider the marriage cove-nant as a sacrament or means of grace. The big idea is that God is so committed to marriage that a couple who seeks to live faithfully for God and one another in covenant is blessed by God with an outpouring of His grace through the Holy Spirit to help them live in love.

The reason many marriages struggle (and even fail) is that they are more of a contract than a covenant. Contracts are needed for professional relationships at work. However, when we bring contractual thinking into marriage, it can result in tense negotiations, demands, pressure to perform, perfor-mance reviews, and punishment for failure to meet demands. Some examples might help you see this in your own marriage. In a counseling session, a husband admitted to committing adultery, and when confronted, he defended himself by blam-ing his wife for not giving him as much sex as he wanted. He told her, "You owed me, and now we are even." Another cou-ple explained during a counseling session that the root of their marriage problems was continual selfishness as every time one of them asked the other for help or a favor, the response was always, "What's in it for me?" The most dysfunctional exam-ple was a couple who literally made job descriptions for each other and gave each other performance reviews at the end of each week. If the husband did what the wife demanded, then he got sex, and if she did what he demanded, then she got paid an allowance to spend as she pleased. They wrongly took

6 Jeremiah 3; 31:31–33; Isaiah 54:5; 62:5; Ezekiel 16; Hosea 2

7 Ephesians 5:22–32; Galatians 4:26–28; 2 Corinthians 11:2; Revelation 19:7–10; 21:9–21; 22:17

their work life and brought it home, treating one another like employees instead of spouses.

To win at home and at work, God's people need to learn about both covenants and contracts. People who only have covenant relationships tend to win at home but lose at work. People who only have contractual relationships tend to win at work but lose at home. People who have contractual relationships at work and covenantal relationships at home tend to win at both. The following table is a summary of the differences between contractual and covenantal relationships:

CONTRACT	vs	COVENANT
Between 2 people		Between 3 people (God, husband, wife)
I seek my will		We seek God's will
You serve me		We serve each other
Performance is recorded		No record of wrongs is kept
Failure is punished		Failure was punished at the cross
Win-lose		Win-win
A professional relationship		A personal relationship

As Hebrews, the couple in the Song of Songs would have been well-aware of the covenant of marriage as they had been taught from the Old Testament. We can use their marriage as a case study from which to learn positive and negative lessons for our own marriage. It is vitally important that we think covenantally about how we can love and serve our spouse, not contractually about what they can do for us. If either the husband or wife reads Song of Songs while putting together a job description for their spouse, then the entire point of marriage and this book of the Bible will be missed. Our goal is not to help you negotiate your contract but to nurture your covenant.

> **IT IS VITALLY IMPORTANT THAT WE THINK COVENANTALLY ABOUT HOW WE CAN LOVE AND SERVE OUR SPOUSE, NOT CONTRACTUALLY ABOUT WHAT THEY CAN DO FOR US.**

Liberating the Ladies

To open the book, the wife (Abbi) speaks first. She is the more passionate communicator in their relationship, contrary to much bad Bible teaching, religious tradition, and cultures that are more modest than God. She speaks firstly, she speaks frequently, and she speaks sensually. Throughout the book, she knows what she wants and says what she likes. It may shock religious folks, but the Bible records the flirtatious invitation of a woman to be kissed for reasons beyond the health benefits that include boosting the immune system and burning two calories. Her flirtation continues, as she says that being with her man is intoxicating like wine and as erotic as the fragrant cologne that surrounds him. She is very obviously excited about being married and going to bed with her husband. In this, we see that while men are genitally aroused, women are generally aroused—everything from his appearance to his character draws her toward him.

To begin, Abbi says she is drawn to Solomon both internally and externally. Internally, she is drawn to the strength of his character. He's a good man with a reputation or "name" that she finds pleasing and fragrant. He is the kind of man with whom all sensible "young women love" to be in a romantic relationship.

Externally, Abbi likes the way his breath and body smell, and throughout the book she is very clear to communicate that she finds him "handsome." For the guys, it's always a good idea to keep up with grooming. Most women prefer two eyebrows instead of one, a man who does not look like he snorted a cat because of all the fur coming out of his nose and ears, breath that does not smell like a garbage can, and a body that has a healthy relationship with soap and water. In addition, wearing pants instead of pajamas to the store, owning at least one shirt with buttons, and clipping your fingernails so you do not feel like the son of Wolverine in the bedroom are also recommended.

Many men complain that their wives are not this forward or free in the bedroom, but they overlook their own character outside the bedroom. The guy who is harsh, rarely home, grumpy, distant, and selfish may not see his role in his wife's lack of desire for physical intimacy. When he spends too much money on his hobbies, refuses emotional and spiritual connection, and won't lead each member of the family, then he has forgotten the simple fact that most of the problems *in* the bedroom are caused by problems *outside* the bedroom. Oftentimes, the solution is not for the husband to improve his sexual techniques, as if he were competing for scores from Olympic judges, but instead to cultivate better character. Your wife wants to be proud of you, and if she's proud of you, then she's more likely to want to be with you. Many men fixate on what their wives will do in the bedroom, but most women are focused first on who he is outside the bedroom. Think about it this way: foreplay includes reading your Bible, praying, raising your hands during worship in church, doing the dishes, apologizing when you are wrong, putting the toilet seat down so she is not routinely baptized in the middle of the night, and not having the emotional disposition of an active volcano. To state it plainly, the reason Abbi wants to sleep in the same bed with her man is because she feels safe with his character and served by his effort to look and smell different than the guy in the middle of the evolutionary chart they had on the wall in our public school.

As Abbi contemplates their special night of sizzling sex, most English translations say she was looking forward to their lovemaking because he had worked hard to "draw" her to himself. Like gravity, his character drew her in.

There are four ways to move a person:

- We can *push* them. This happens in domineering, abusive, threatening, and punishing relationships.
- We can *carry* them. This happens in enabling, co-dependent, and unhealthy relationships.
- We can *drag* them. This happens in inconsiderate, controlling, and selfish relationships.
- We can *draw* them. This happens in loving, healthy, safe, and fun relationships.

Solomon's character draws Abbi to him. Although she is attracted to her man, excited to be with him, and overt and honest with him, there is still one big problem she talks through with her friends. She is feeling self-conscious and unattractive, so she names her insecurities. Like Cinderella, she does not fit her culture's stereotypical definition of beauty.

Abbi's mother and brothers are mentioned in the book but not her father. In addition, she was poor. Apparently, Abbi had no dad, and she worked outside in the hot sun, which left her dirty, sweaty, and sunburned. Abbi's dark hair (like goat hair tents, we read) was probably in a ponytail or tied up in some other way most days while she worked. To help provide for her family, this young woman spent her days with dirt under her fingernails and callouses on her hands.

Various cultures have differing standards of beauty. In Abbi's culture, the wealthy women stayed home to keep their skin pale while being tended to by their servants, not working away from home sweating in the sun and getting a farmer's tan.

As we have learned, God does not give us a standard of beauty; rather, He gives us our spouse as our standard for beauty not to be compared to anyone else. Job 31:1 echoes this idea by saying, "I made a covenant with my eyes not to look lustfully."

We live in the most difficult period of human history to keep our eyes from seeing what is not good for our souls or marriages. We now have screens in our homes, cars, offices, and phones that are constantly bombarding us with lustful images luring us to covet. Additionally, our over-sexualized culture encourages people to adorn themselves with underwear as outerwear. There is a constant battle for our eyes, which is really a spiritual war for the health of our marriages. The world's system continually and aggressively tries to make us insecure about our own appearances, dissatisfied with our spouses, and lustful after anyone other than the one person with whom God permits our sexual activity.

In the Song of Songs, this passionate young woman was transitioning from being a peasant to a princess, and she was insecure about her appearance. Imagine how much more difficult this is in our day with photoshop and social media? Everyone has imperfections, of which they are likely well aware. To serve our spouses, it's a good idea for us to be careful stewards of our health with things like a wholesome diet and lifestyle, including exercise, grooming, and dressing in ways that prepare and present our bodies for our spouses.

I (Grace) know that as women, we see all our flaws, so our husbands don't need to point them out. Rather, compliments and encouragement make us want to keep presenting ourselves as feminine and desirable. It is easy for us to get discouraged with the many life and body changes we go through with pregnancy, aging, and hormonal imbalances, but if a wife is the standard of beauty for her husband, then she will still feel free and safe in his arms.

Healthy Family and Friends

Notice the inclusion of close family and friends who care for the woman throughout the book. In any romantic relationship, a good guy will get to know the people who love the woman he is falling in love with early in their relationship.

He will be overt, not hiding who he is or avoiding getting to know them, as is illustrated throughout the Song of Songs. Conversely, a bad guy will avoid the people who care for the woman, isolate her, and make their relationship covert, which leaves her in harm's way. In the Song of Songs, the people who know Abbi also know Solomon, and the people who love her also love him; they give their approval and advice throughout their relationship. This puts her in a safe place with a safe man.

The "friends" who speak approvingly of their relationship are the couple's wise counsel. In the wisdom book of Proverbs, which Solomon also wrote, much is said about wisdom and seeking wise counsel. Every couple needs wise counsel, including family or friends, rather than venting to the people around us, dragging our immediate family into our marriages and sex lives, or betraying privacy and posting our private matters publicly online. Since many couples do not have wise, godly, and healthy extended family members, God's family in a local church is the best place to find spiritual family and friends who share your values and can walk with you wisely and discreetly. We cannot stress this enough. We love the local church, and while every church family has its problems (just like any family), the Bible is clear that it's not good to be alone. God's people must not forsake regularly gathering together (see Hebrews 10:25).

Knowing that Solomon is busy shepherding the nation as Israel's king, Abbi laments having to share so much of her man's time and energy with his job. So she meets him for lunch but is careful not to do so in a way that resembles the prostitutes, who also pursued men working away from home. She is persistent and passionate in a way that is godly and not like the godless women of the pagan people surround Israel. She is creating sacred time together and speaking honestly about her desires and fears for their relationship.

Protecting Priorities

One perennially popular myth regarding romance is that it happens naturally and without effort. People often think of this effortless romance as finding their "soul mate"—that one person with whom they will connect and fit without even trying. This powerful myth began in ungodly ancient Greek mythology and was popularized by Plato. It also has expressions in Hinduism and Buddhism but not in Judaism or Christianity. It was said that two married people were conjoined at the rear, and contained within each couple was an entire gender spectrum of three sexes, genders, and genitalia—male, female, and androgynous. The Greek god Zeus became angry and cut humans in half, sending them to live lonely, disconnected, and separated lives. Ever since, people have been seeking their "soul mate"—literally the one person who has the other half of their shared soul. Hinduism teaches that you might not find that person in this life, but through multiple incarnations, you may finally get it right.

Nothing could be further from the Christian faith or the truth. We do not have a "soul mate." People no more "fall in love" than they fall into health or wisdom. It takes work to have a good marriage and overcome the obstacles that are always working against us. In this section of the Song of Songs, the couple is dealing with the realities of life. Solomon is busy at work, and Abbi's life is full of responsibilities that are crowding out their time and energy. Their romantic discussion includes the very practical matter of when and where to meet. In other words, they are scheduling time together. Abbi says she does not want to be like an immoral woman who is chasing a man around, so she invites Solomon to make their relationship a priority by letting her know what his schedule is and when and where they can get time together.

We were not great at this early in our marriage, and it cost us dearly. Between a lot of work in planting a church, starting a church in our living room (that God grew and led to almost 10,000 baptisms!), adding five kids, plus extended family, friends, and everyone and everything else, our lives felt like an avalanche we were buried under, spending every waking moment seeking to shovel out to no avail.

We were so busy working *in* our marriage that we did not work *on* our marriage. We would never have lived in a home that was not designed by an architect for health and safety, but somehow, we had moved our family into a life that was not intentionally architected. That needed to change, and *four little things made an enormous difference.*

First, we got a *shared digital calendar* so that our lives and schedules were organized and together as one. It's hard to be "one" as God says if you do not intentionally and practically schedule your life together.

Second, we scheduled *a weekly sync meeting* to discuss the practical details of life that need to be talked through, prayed about, planned for, and put in the budget and on the calendar. This was different than our weekly date night, where we planned something fun and romantic to build our friendship. We learned the hard way that when we did not have a sync meeting, our date night would turn into a sync meeting, which was as romantic as a staff meeting at work. The benefits of the sync meeting include knowing how to pray for each other every day, knowing that certain days will be more exhausting or stressful so we can serve and give grace to one another, and being able to check in throughout the day with a call or text to see how things are going because we know what is going on. The sync meeting is especially helpful to get a unified plan for Sabbath days, holidays, vacations, and busy seasons, such as when our three boys played as many combined baseball games as a Major League team (and needed to be driven to every game and practice).

Third, we started spending time each year on *a vision retreat*. During this special time, we prayed together and planned out our year as best we could according to our priorities, which are:

1. Healthy relationship with God as Christians
2. Healthy relationship with each other as a married couple
3. Healthy relationship with each of our children as parents
4. Healthy work-life balance as employees at work
5. Healthy relationship with extended family members and close Christian friends

After decades of pastoral ministry, one of the most frequent mistakes we see Christian couples make is collapsing priorities 2 and 3 into a general category called "family." To be sure, children are a blessing, and God cares greatly for our families. We fully believe this as the parents of five children. However, we were married before we had children in our home, and we want to remain married after our children leave our home. In the Song of Songs, the focus is on marriage, and there is no mention of children.

> **IN THE SONG OF SONGS, THE FOCUS IS ON MARRIAGE, AND THERE IS NO MENTION OF CHILDREN.**

When children overtake a marriage as the constant priority, at least two painful things occur. First, the spouses feel neglected and even jealous of the children because the marriage is not the priority it should be. Second, when the children leave home, the glue that held the marriage together loses its connectivity. The couple will often fall apart or start demanding that their grown children give them grandchildren, because their marriage cannot function with just the two of them. We are of the age where we see many Christian marriages implode as children leave home. We love our children, but our marriage is our priority over them. One of the best things we can do for our grown children is model for them a healthy marriage and a secure set of parents they can depend on and not have to worry about. We want the same for you.

If you have children, the goal is to raise and then launch them to build their own marriages, enjoy their own children, and look forward to their futures. If your marriage is broken, then your children will likely keep looking back in concern for *your* marriage, and their burden for you will hinder their ability to pour energy into their own marriages and families, which then risks extending your unhealthy marriage patterns into generations of your family's future legacy. The best thing you can do in every season of your marriage for you, your spouse, and your children is to make your relationship with God and your spouse your top two priorities so that you and your marriage are healthy and a blessing rather than a burden for your kids and grandkids.

Fourth, we learned to *put fun on the calendar.* I (Mark) tend to be more stressed than Grace. For me to change my pace, I need to change my place. To give my mind a break, I need to break away from our routine. Grace is different, and we've had to learn how to spend Sabbath and vacation together through trial and error. For me, always having fun on the calendar is a necessity even if it's simple. I need to know that in addition to at least one regular weekly date, we have future plans to do a romantic overnight together, go on a trip, and have a relaxing and romantic adventure. I'm also the party planner for the kids; arranging fun and making memories is what I love to do. Life will not automatically provide you breaks and memories, so you need to create these sacred windows of opportunity on the calendar and in the budget. In the Song of Songs, this is what Abbi is speaking about—inviting Solomon to take her away, which is the very thing that happens in the next chapter. Before we learn about En Gedi, though, we first have an intimate exercise for you.

The goal of our time together learning God's Word is not just information but also application that leads to transformation. Our goal is to encourage you both to connect with God and each other to deepen and strengthen those relationships.

When you sit down to discuss these questions face-to-face, please look each other in the eye. Much of marriage is shoulder-to shoulder getting things done. When we are fighting, we are back-to-back, not looking at one another or drawing each other in. The key to a healthy, holy, and happy marriage is getting lots of face-to-face time, looking one another in the eye, and building an intimate friendship. The default we easily fall into is a shoulder-to-shoulder relationship, and when we are stuck there for too long, we slip into back-to-back. The only way out is to get time to discuss and pray kindly and lovingly face-to-face. Please make this your habit for these discussion times.

Lastly, please know we love you and are praying for you!

FACE-TO-FACE QUESTIONS
for Couple Discussion

1. How are you doing at open and honest communication about your passionate desires and fearful insecurities in your relationship? What needs to be said in a kind, loving, and inviting way?

2. What are your honest initial thoughts about the woman speaking first, speaking most, and being passionate and strongly vocal about her desires and concerns for their relationship?

3. Who are the friends you want to be wise counsel in your life? What people have a voice into your relationship who are not wise and should not be invited into the details and decision-making of your marriage, such as unhealthy friends or extended family?

4. Is there anything in your spouse's character that you can encourage and show gratitude for? Is there anything in your spouse's character that you can lovingly and kindly request improvement on, responding humbly and not defensively?

5. When will you have a shared calendar, weekly sync meeting, and weekly date? How are you doing at making your relationship a priority in relation to work and other responsibilities?

6. How can you pray for each other this week?

Chapter 2

EN GEDI
1:8–2:7

Friends

1:8 If you do not know, most beautiful of women,
follow the tracks of the sheep
and graze your young goats
by the tents of the shepherds.

He

9 I liken you, my darling, to a mare
among Pharaoh's chariot horses.

10 Your cheeks are beautiful with earrings,
your neck with strings of jewels.

11 We will make you earrings of gold,
studded with silver.

She

12 While the king was at his table,
my perfume spread its fragrance.

13 My beloved is to me a sachet of myrrh
resting between my breasts.

14 My beloved is to me a cluster of henna blossoms
from the vineyards of En Gedi.

He

15 How beautiful you are, my darling!
Oh, how beautiful!
Your eyes are doves.

She

16 How handsome you are, my beloved!
Oh, how charming!
And our bed is verdant.

He

17 The beams of our house are cedars;
our rafters are firs.

She

2:1 I am a rose of Sharon,
a lily of the valleys.

He

2 Like a lily among thorns
is my darling among the young women.

She

3 Like an apple tree among the trees of the forest
is my beloved among the young men.
I delight to sit in his shade,
and his fruit is sweet to my taste.
4 Let him lead me to the banquet hall,
and let his banner over me be love.
5 Strengthen me with raisins,
refresh me with apples,
for I am faint with love.

6 His left arm is under my head,
and his right arm embraces me.

7 Daughters of Jerusalem, I charge you
by the gazelles and by the does of the field:
Do not arouse or awaken love
until it so desires.

———

There once was a couple we were trying to help who was in real marital crisis. The husband was very overextended at work, and the wife was terribly busy at home with young children and helping to care for her aging parents. Their marriage was functional but not fun. They were roommates but not bonded together like a married couple should be. He was working hard to provide financially but was not providing much emotionally or spiritually. To make matters worse, the husband was so controlling of their finances that he thought spending money on fun and making memories was wasteful. His wife felt discouraged by his long hours at work and the fact that as their net-worth increased, her self-worth decreased.

Their story is common as finances are consistently listed as the biggest marital stressors. As we talked to this typical couple, it seemed obvious that they needed to spend some money to get time away together on romantic dates and trips and to invest not just in their retirement but also their romance. The problem was they had different money personalities.

While financial experts use various terms, there are seven general money personalities:

1. The Hoarder: "Money gives me security."
2. The Spender: "Money gives me rewards."
3. The Avoider: "Money and bills stress me out."

4. The Hater: "Money is evil and dangerous."
5. The Manipulator: "Money buys me influence/control."
6. The Show-Off: "Money gives me status through possessions."
7. The Giver: "Money is how I show God and people love."[x]

The husband was a hoarder and an avoider. Growing up extremely poor with a single mother, he did not learn about money, so he didn't like to talk about it. He was very tight with finances and put a lot of pressure on his wife to spend next to nothing. But she was a spender and a giver. She liked to give gifts to people and had no problem spending money on building their marriage relationship.

When we sat down to discuss different things that they could do to have fun, spend time together, and make memories, she was eager to share her list of ideas. At the top of her list were spa days, dinner dates, trips, updating the furniture in their bedroom to make it romantic, and getting some work done on their bathroom to give it a vacation feel. Some of her ideas had a big price tag, and others came with less expense. She did not care much how much was spent but rather that her husband showed he cared with some spending.

The wife's face sank when her husband said he could not afford the money for such "luxuries." The truth is, he had a fantastic job and a good income, and because they were frugal, they had a lot of money in the bank and no debt beyond their mortgage. He was thinking about the pain of spending money, while she was thinking about joy of sharing memories.

Eventually, we asked him how much a good divorce attorney was and how much they would have to spend to get divorced. We had him sketch out on paper where they would be financially if their dying marriage did not survive. Once he calculated the staggering amount, he looked up at his wife, apologized, said he loved her, and committed to spend the money on their current marriage and not a future divorce. That was a drastic exercise, but it made him realize his marriage was a wise investment. In that moment, something healed in their relationship. He told her he would love to go on adventures, have dates, take trips, and make memories with her. Then he apologized for having been too fixated on money. The husband promised he would set aside a percentage of the budget for his wife to help other people and spend on planning fun for them as well. Every month, he put money aside and trusted her do with it as she pleased. Grateful for his heart change, she stewarded the money well, gave to God, helped others, and made sure they always had fun on the calendar to look forward to as a way of building their marriage friendship.

As an aside, we would also warn you to be incredibly careful about accepting money from family or friends with any strings attached. If you've ever seen a puppet show, the strings on the puppet belong to the puppet master who uses them to control the puppet. Sadly, many people, especially parents and grandparents, offer money with strings so they can be the puppet masters in your marriage. As a married couple, God expects *you* to make the decisions for your family. Extended family and friends whom you respect and invite into your life as wise counsel can give you their advice to help you make your own decisions. However, some people want to make the decisions for your family, so they give money to control things such as where you live, how you vacation, where your children attend school, and which church you join. That kind of giving is not grace based but is manipulative and controlling. The couple we just examined had a relative who would give money to the husband with a lot of demands regarding how it was to be spent, which ultimately contributed to his failure to be generous with his wife and their marriage.

Most couples fall in love by planning and enjoying fun adventures together. Sadly, the pain often comes when the planning stops, and we fall into the rut of our marital routine. We get so busy doing the dishes, walking the dog, and folding the laundry that we forget to make plans, have fun, and make the Song of Songs sing again.

> **MOST COUPLES FALL IN LOVE BY PLANNING AND ENJOYING FUN ADVENTURES TOGETHER. SADLY, THE PAIN OFTEN COMES WHEN THE PLANNING STOPS, AND WE FALL INTO THE RUT OF OUR MARITAL ROUTINE.**

In this section of the Song of Songs, Solomon and Abbi get advice from wise counsel, flirt with one another, and plan an epic trip to their favorite romantic destination, En Gedi. He also spends some money to buy her nice jewelry to show her she is a priority in his heart, life, budget, and schedule. James 1:22 says, "Do not deceive yourselves by just listening to his word; instead, put it into practice" (GNT). Is that what you do? Where are some of the favorite places you have gone together? Where were your favorite memories made?

I (Mark) have a lot of amazing memories I share with Grace. Growing up in a working-class family with five kids, I did not travel much, because my dad was always working construction to feed our family. We lived next to an airport, and as the planes flew over our house, I often looked up, wondering where they were going and longing for the day when I could see the nation and world. As a pastor, I have been blessed to visit much of America and somewhere around two dozen nations. Whenever possible, I have taken Grace and our five kids with me so that we could explore the world together. One of my favorite trips, however, did not involve the kids. To celebrate our 50th birthdays, we went to Germany to tour the historical sites of Martin and Katherine Luther and learn more about their marriage and ministry. We finished the trip on the romantic lower Rhine River. We stayed in an old inn overlooking the water and spent days traveling by ferry to visit small towns. We sat outside to eat meals, talked without interruption, explored museums, hiked to old churches, and popped into artisan shops. We had no children, no schedule, and no work. I loved having Grace all to myself, waking up whenever we wanted, going wherever we wanted, and doing whatever we wanted with the sun kissing our faces.

A favorite trip in the US for me (Grace) was a short flight to Montana. We stayed in a lodge on a lake, took walks in town, went boating, sat out at night by the bonfire, slept in, did a Vision Retreat (led by Jimmy Evans), explored towns and antique stores, had dinner with a pastor and his wife, ate at local eateries, and went to Glacier National Park (including rafting on the river). It was so fun being together as a couple and experiencing a variety of scenery and activities.

Wise Counsel

Throughout the Song of Songs, the "friends" continue to speak into the relationship. These friends are what Proverbs calls wise counsel. Any couple who does not have close relationships with godly people is not in a healthy place, because there is no one to speak into their life together. Worse still, welcoming your extended family, coworkers, or unhealthy people to know about or speak into your relationship is generally a bad thing to do. Even worse is inviting ungodly or unhealthy people to have a view and a voice into your marriage.

For someone to be wise counsel, you need to know they are wise, and they need to know they are counsel. A wise person lives by the power of the Holy Spirit, knows the Bible, embraces reality, has empathy for others, takes responsibility for themselves, is humble enough to learn and repent, and thinks in terms of legacy. Different people have wisdom in different areas, which is why your marriage is best served by a "multitude of counselors."[8]

Who are the good people for you to seek wise counsel from in various areas such as Scripture, marriage, finances, parenting, scheduling, health, and work? Most of the time, these people are found in a good church as you get connected, serve, and make relationships with other couples. Who are the older couples walking ahead of you who could serve as wise counsel for you? Who are the couples in your life stage who can walk alongside you as friends and wise counsel? Who are the singles and couples younger than you and walking behind you for whom you can serve as wise counsel?

Once you have identified a small list of people to invite to be your wise counsel, then you should pray a lot as a couple about approaching them and both agree that you feel safe with them seeing and speaking into your marriage. Once that list is finished, you need to meet with the people you want to serve as your wise counsel and ask if you could learn from them because you respect them. As a general rule, you should not ask for a lot of their time; rather, ask if you can schedule time with them when you get stuck and need advice to get unstuck. When you meet with them,

8 Proverbs 11:4 NKJV

arrive on time, come prepared with a list of questions, be respect-ful, listen a lot, take notes, and then take action on what they tell you to do. You should also ask them for any other resources they would recommend, such as a class, book, podcast, or other help that you can take responsibility for and integrate into your life. Wise people do not want to waste their time, but they do want to invest it. If you do not burden them very much, and you act on their counsel with humility and gratitude, then wise people tend to be immensely helpful for a long time.

The people you welcome into your relationship as a couple will either help or hinder your marriage's health. This section begins with the couple's wise counsel giving good advice to help them build their intimacy by encouraging mutual pursuit between the man and woman.

Grace and I have wise counsel for us as individuals and as a couple. We do not confide in or seek counsel from people whom we do not agree should be invited to see and speak into our marriage. Only godly men should serve as wise counsel for a husband, and only godly women should serve as wise counsel for a wife. Only a mutually trusted and agreed upon couple in a good marriage should serve as wise counsel for your marriage. The recurrence of the "friends" throughout the Song of Songs shows the importance of godly, safe, and wise relationships with people who love God, love us, and help us walk together in God's will for our marriage.

Compliments and Nicknames

One of the first things we learn after opening a bank account is the difference between a deposit and a withdrawal. If you do not keep your deposits greater than your withdrawals, then you will bankrupt your account, which can lead to the bank ultimately closing your account altogether. A marriage is a bit like a bank. Compliments are deposits, and criticisms are withdrawals. If we criticize more than we compliment, then we can bankrupt the marriage account, possibly even causing our spouse to close their heart to us. The key to keeping the marriage account full is being intentional about making frequent deposits in the form of sincere compliments.

> **A MARRIAGE IS A BIT LIKE A BANK. COMPLIMENTS ARE DEPOSITS, AND CRITICISMS ARE WITHDRAWALS.**

We see the husband and wife compliment one another throughout the Song of Songs. In this section, the references to sheep and goats, along with mares and horses, may not immediately register in our imagination unless you grew up on a farm, but that's what is happening. The man gives specific compliments about what he finds beautiful and delightful about his beloved. Having 12,000 magnificent Egyptian horses and 1,400 chariots as King of Israel, he likens her to a beautiful mare that stands alone, meaning Abbi is the kind of woman that every man wishes they could be with forever. If you grew up in a city like us, then the only thing we know about horses is that we don't know much about horses. From what we can tell, a horse is a boy, and a mare is a girl. If you are a boy horse hanging out with 11,999 guy horses and one girl horse gallops in, then she is going to cause quite a stir, and that's the gist of this farm flirtation. If you think he's calling himself a stud that gets really excited around his mare, then you get the point of this ranching romance.

Nicknames are one of the most powerful ways we make deposits and withdrawals in our marriage accounts. We tend to give nicknames to the people we love or the ones we dislike the most, and sadly, people often have both kinds for their spouses. Negative, critical nicknames are curses used to trigger deep hurt in spouses and establish an identity for them that is unchanging, hopeless, and discouraging. Positive, complimentary nicknames lift our spouses up, encourage them, and bless them.

Over the years, we've heard of some fun nicknames with couples. We know husbands referred to as "hubby," "dude of dudes," "my man," "cowboy," "big sexy," the "stud," "stud muffin," "fuzzy buddy," "Mr. Dreamy," and "best friend." We also know wives referred to as "sweetie pie," "honey," the "curvy cutie," "hot momma," "princess," the "queen," and "beauty." Solomon gives Abbi the nicknames "my beloved" and "my darling" and promises to give her gifts of jewelry that he has picked out to remind her of his affection and devotion.

How we see ourselves is often through the eyes of our spouse. This viewpoint can be a wonderful or woeful reality depending upon how our spouse chooses to see us. When Abbi says, "I am a rose of Sharon, a lily of the valleys" (2:1), she explains that she sees herself as unattractive and not unique, special, or valuable. She compares herself to the rose of Sharon, a common wildflower that grew like a weed. When Solomon says, "Like a lily among thorns is my darling among the young women" (2:2), he is inviting her to see herself through his eyes,

> **HOW WE SEE OURSELVES IS OFTEN THROUGH THE EYES OF OUR SPOUSE.**

with other women as thorns and her as a lovely lily. Whether we are flirting with and complimenting our spouses or fighting with and criticizing our spouses, we are inviting them to see themselves through our eyes.

Here are some examples to get you started:

- I love you because _____.

- What I most appreciate about you is _____.

- The reason I fell in love with you was because _____.

- My favorite memories with you are _____.

- What makes you special is _____.

- What I look forward to most in our future together is _____.

- Thank you for _____.

The Bible talks a lot about sowing and reaping. In marriage, this principle is constantly at play. If you raise your voice to your spouse, then you will probably get a raised voice in return. If you sweetly hug your spouse, then you will probably get a hug in response. The principle of sowing and reaping appears throughout the Song of Songs as the man and woman take turns speaking to one another, complimenting one another, and flirting with one another.

This is especially true if either party was bullied or grew up in a verbally abusive home. Tragically, some negative nicknames, criticisms, and vicious voices ring so loud in our ears throughout our lives that only a steady echo of encouraging blessings can drown out the discouraging curses.

For a woman to be free, she needs to feel safe. The freedom of this woman is in large part attributable to her trust in the character of her man. When Abbi says, "Let his banner over me be love" (2:4), it is a military term taken from the battlefield. When ancient nations would go to war in hand-to-hand combat, the soldiers would get scattered, so a large banner or flag of their nation would be lifted high above the battlefield. Vulnerable soldiers simply needed to look up to the flag or banner, and it pointed them to the place of safety from the raging war. Abbi is saying that Solomon loves her, and he's tough for her but also tender with her. He will not fight *with* her, but he will fight *for* her. If she stays close to him, then he will lead her wisely, cherish her deeply, provide for her generously, and protect her fiercely. In this way, he is a bit like Jesus, who is both a Lion and a Lamb.[9] As a Lion, Jesus goes to war with Satan and demons to defend us. As a Lamb, Jesus is tender and kind with us. In Hell, Jesus rules as Lion. In Heaven, Jesus rules as Lamb. As both a tough Lion for us and tender Lamb with us, His banner over His bride, the Church, is "love." In this section of the Song of Songs, Abbi is saying her man reminds her of our God-Man.

The opposite of a good man is one who is harsh with his wife. Colossians 3:19 says, "Husbands, love your wives and do not be harsh with them." First Peter 3:7 adds, "Likewise, husbands, live with your wives in an understanding way, showing honor to the woman as the weaker vessel, since they are heirs with you of the grace of life, so that your prayers may not be hindered" (ESV). A husband can yell louder and push harder than his wife, and an evil man will use his strength to

---

9 See Revelation 5:5–6.

dominate his wife. A good man will use his power to defend his wife. That's the trust every woman needs in her man.

I (Mark) grew up in a neighborhood with gangs, drugs, and prostitution nearby. I had a knife pulled on me for the first time when I was in elementary school, so I learned to be constantly aware of my surroundings and safety. Grace grew up a bit more naïve, and not having any brothers, she did not really understand the common, messed up male mindset. As soon as we started hanging out as friends, I became protective of her. For example, one time we were holding hands on a walk, and I moved to the side closest to the road. She asked why I did that, and I told her I needed to be closest to the road so that if a car swerved, I would get hit instead of her. Another time, a hostess seated us at a restaurant, and I asked for the corner booth. I motioned for Grace to slide in so I could be on the edge closest to the door. She asked why I did that, and I explained I needed to see who was coming in and out so I could protect her from any potential danger. At first, Grace thought I was a little over the top, but through the years she's come to understand that her safety is my priority, which I later extended to our children once we were blessed to be parents.

A Sachet of Myrrh Resting Between My Breasts?

In response to her manly man, Abbi speaks in a very flirtatious and even erotic way by saying she wants him to rest his head between her breasts. God's Word is frank without being crass, but some religious people find it too honest, which has led to some odd and funny interpretations throughout church history. For example, some religious leaders have said this is a metaphorical reference to the Shekinah glory between the two cherubim angels that stood over the Ark of the Covenant in the Tabernacle, or that the two breasts are the Old and New Covenants that bring us the pure milk of the Word, and the sachet of myrrh is Christ between them. This part of the anatomy is mentioned multiple times in the Song of Songs and should remind religious folks that if they are more conservative than God, then it's a good idea to scoot to the left.

There are two ways God's people can err in relation to sex. The first way is going far into sin. This is what happens in the world, which causes people in the Church to overreact to the world rather than returning to the Word. The second error and sad result happens when the Church teaches on sex but does not go far enough into the freedoms and pleasures God intends for a husband and wife. Instead of naming all that God allows and explaining why the best sex is within the protective limits of God's commands, much Christian teaching on sex focuses on what God forbids and allegorizes what God says about the freedoms of sex, because they believe they should be able to draw the line and then tell God where it is. The Bible is clear on the heart and actions of sexual sin, so we don't need to add to God's Word either by pushing it forward like the world does or pulling it back like the Church does. If a godly wife speaks repeatedly of her body and the husband does the same throughout a book of the Bible, then believers have God's permission to do the same.

> **MUCH CHRISTIAN TEACHING ON SEX FOCUSES ON WHAT GOD FORBIDS AND ALLEGORIZES WHAT GOD SAYS ABOUT THE FREEDOMS OF SEX, BECAUSE THEY BELIEVE THEY SHOULD BE ABLE TO DRAW THE LINE AND THEN TELL GOD WHERE IT IS.**

En Gedi

In their fun flirtation, Abbi mentions a place called En Gedi. The man and woman lived in a barren desert, but within it was a beautiful oasis that still exists to this day. We personally visited it on a trip to Israel. Out of that parched, barren desert springs forth fresh water that feeds an oasis of lush plants covered by ample shade. Apparently, this was one of Abbi's favorite places to spend time with her beloved. The application for us is that we need to find ways to make En Gedi places in our relationships. These places include our bedrooms, homes, and vacation getaways where we can relax, sabbath, make memories, and build our relationships.

> **WE NEED TO FIND WAYS TO MAKE EN GEDI PLACES IN OUR RELATIONSHIPS.**

A romantic retreat is precisely what happens in this section of the Song of Songs. In addition to going to En Gedi, Abbi talks about having En Gedi in their home by saying, "Our bed is verdant" (1:16). Solomon replies, "The beams of our house are cedars; our rafters are firs" (1:17). Since heaven is our forever home and it will be a perfect place, we should set up our homes as best we can to practice for our eternal homecoming.

When our kids were little, we told them our bedroom was set apart and not for them. We had a lock on the door so they would not walk in unexpectedly to discover how they got here, and we asked them to knock before entering. The kids did not play in our bedroom, and as a result, it was not covered in crackers, half-eaten lollipops, or action figures like the rest of the house. We do not bring our laptops to our bedroom, because it's not a place for work. In the Bible, for something to be holy, it means it is set apart for a specific use, and we wanted our bedroom to be holy and set apart for us to connect and rest. We set up our bedroom and our bathroom as a place to sneak away for a little slice of En Gedi at night once the kids went to bed. This is an important discussion to have: what does En Gedi look like at home and away from home for your marriage?

For me (Mark), the outdoor space is just as important as the indoor space. For the first decades of our marriage, I suffered from Seasonal Affective Disorder (a type of depression). The long, wet, and dark winters took a physical and emotional toll on me, and I spent so much time checking the weather app on my phone and planning trips to sunny places that the kids started joking that I was "solar powered." Today, living in Arizona has been one of the greatest blessings in my life. I love to study outside, eat outside, hike outside, and sit by the fire in the cool nights outside. One of my favorite things is simply holding Grace's hand and going for a walk in our neighborhood as we enjoy the desert sunshine and fresh air. Inside, I've always liked having my library and study at home so that my family sees me study the Bible and has access to my books so they can study for themselves. And I must always have fun on the calendar. I am the one in our family who is always asking where everyone wants to go and what memories they want to make. From day trips to exotic trips around the globe, I love to have En Gedi on the calendar so we always have something to look forward to.

For me (Grace), I had to get creative in our first dozen years of marriage since we didn't have a slush fund to pull from. With all the "decorating on a budget" resources we have now, it's much easier to create restful places at home. I had to work on getting organized (not my natural gifting) and make it a priority to arrange our room and bathroom into a place of fun and beauty. Even having fun dates at home that transitioned our room into a "vacation" destination with beach towels (minus the sand, of course), picnics, fruity drinks, music, and fun, sexy attire served as a getaway when we couldn't actually get away. I loved all the trips we were blessed to take as well, and Mark was great at planning those for us. I researched the areas and used my gift of saving money on lodging and activities, and Mark would dream about what we both wanted to do together to build new memories. We also asked people who wanted to give us gifts for holidays and birthdays to give us gift cards to restaurants and movie theaters so we could use them for date nights. The point is to get resourceful if finances are tight; find creative and fun ways not only to date until you are married but also to continue dating after you are married.

What would it look like for you to go to En Gedi and bring En Gedi home? Intentionally planning and organizing your home is an effective way to start. Some years ago, after we taught this section of the Song of Songs, a couple scheduled a counseling meeting at our church. The husband lamented that their sex life was neither free nor frequent. The wife immediately became defensive and said it was his fault. As their disagreement escalated, she explained her frustration that he never put a tub in their private bathroom or a lock on the door to their bedroom. The wife really wanted to spend her nights in the tub sipping wine after putting the kids in bed, and somehow this man who was a contractor never got around to what you would expect to be his highest priority. To make matters worse, on more than one occasion when the couple was intimate, their young kids opened the door and walked in to see mom and dad "wrestling." The hapless husband was one trip away to the hardware store to start singing the Song of Songs with his wife and saving a small fortune on counseling bills for his kids, but he failed to see the obvious and practical solution to their sexual frustrations.

His Fruit Is Sweet to My Taste?

As the couple dream about time away together, things start heating up from their flirting. Someone has said that when it comes to sex, a man is a microwave, and a woman is a crockpot. A man is pretty much ready all the time, and if not, just give him a millisecond, and he can be ready. A woman, however, warms up slowly and stays hot longer. Flirtatious compliments are a good way to warm her up throughout the day, which explains why he gives specific compliments to her, including calling her beautiful and loyal. The mention of doves is noteworthy because they have one mate, they are faithful to one another for their entire lives, and the dove is the symbol of purity and peace. Solomon also says Abbi is like a beautiful lily among thorn bushes in his heart compared to other women.

Using poetic language, Abbi says she looks forward to going to bed with him, having him stroke her body, performing oral sex on him, and being passionate for so long that they will grow tired and possibly need to stop for snacks to refuel, including items that were considered ancient aphrodisiacs. The poetic language is their flirtatious and creative way to be privately frank without being crass or clinical. They neither fall into the kind of language gross guys use in the locker room, nor do they use the clinical terms of a doctor's office.

They also don't discuss body parts the same way our three-year-old child used to do. A healthy married couple has their own poetic ways of speaking intimately while speaking in a way that is neither crass nor clinical.

If you are wondering if we made a typo and mistakenly mentioned terrific oral sex when we really meant to talk about a tyrannosaurus rex, then you need to learn to put the fun back in fundamentalism. This 3,000-year-old book of the Bible has a lot of things that were never made into a Veggie Tale cartoon, and this is perhaps the most obvious reason why. Here's exactly what Abbi says by the inspiration of the same Holy Spirit who inspired Moses to write the Ten Commandments and Paul to pen the doctrine of justification by faith. In Song of Songs 2:3 she says,

> Like an apple tree among the trees of the forest
>> is my beloved among the young men.
> I delight to sit in his shade,
>> and his fruit is sweet to my taste.

Knowing that religious prudes and nerds will want to criticize us for saying what this really means, we will now use an old trick where we quote the experts as our sexperts. Old Testament scholar Joseph Dillow says in the Bible commentary *Solomon on Sex*, "It is possible that here we have a faint and delicate reference to an oral genital caress."[xi] One Bible commentator with more degrees than Fahrenheit says, "She … tells how she delighted to shelter under the lover and to taste his fruit. It would be difficult to read this as anything other than a metaphor for sexual fulfillment. The view that women do not or should not find pleasure in sex, found in cultures both primitive and sophisticated, is plainly not shared by our poet."[xii] In summary, Abbi likes to do things that Solomon also likes her doing.

Song of Songs shows the fullness of their sexual freedom. The couple has pillow talk, caressing, and oral sex in this section and also in another, as well as a marital removal of clothing (striptease?) near the end of the book. These freedoms are not, however, prescribed for every godly marriage. The Bible repeatedly speaks about our consciences, and we are encouraged to honor both God's Word over us and the conscience He placed within us.[10] For Christians, when it comes to debatable things, including the wine they drink and sex illustrated in the Song of Songs, every individual and couple needs to consider the following three categories:

1. Receive: Can I receive this act or action as a gift from God that is not forbidden by His Word or my conscience? If so, then I am free to receive and enjoy it.

2. Reject: Is this something that neither God's Word nor my conscience can receive? If so, then I just reject it.

3. Redeem: Is this something that can be used in a godly or ungodly way, but according to the Bible, it is a freedom, and my conscience is clear to receive this act or action as a gift from God that is good if done rightly?

These questions keep us from imposing freedoms on people whose consciences have not freed them or restricting freedoms from people whose consciences permit them. These questions push us to the Scriptures, prayer, our own consciences, the leading of the Holy Spirit, and loving conversations with our spouses, while also possibly seeking wise

---

10 Romans 2:14–15; 1 Timothy 1:5; 4:2; Titus 1:15

counsel. These same categories of questions can be applied to a host of sexual questions the Bible does not answer but that modern day couples have, which includes the use of sex toys, frankness of pillow talk, various sexual positions and locations, and the intimate use of technology solely between husband and wife when they are separated for extended periods of time, such as a military deployment or business travel. These are not the kinds of things you must do, but they are the kinds of things you are free to discuss and try if you both agree. As we grow in our marriages and build trust, sometimes our consciences change, and things we did not want to try before, we are now interested in trying as our lovemaking is maturing. Like every aspect of marriage, there is change and growth if the relationship is healthy. We started out extremely basic in our freedoms, but as we grew in trust and healing from our past, we were willing to try new things and find new freedoms in our marriage.

The biggest idea in the Song of Songs is that a couple needs to have an ongoing conversation about every aspect of their marital relationship, including sex. Sadly, many Christian couples have lots of conversations about everyone and everything but sex. One of the saddest counseling sessions we've had in our years of marriage ministry happened early in our own marriage, and it was a sober warning. A husband and wife both committed adultery within a few weeks of each other. When their sins became known, they sat down to explain what happened. The

> **THE BIGGEST IDEA IN THE SONG OF SONGS IS THAT A COUPLE NEEDS TO HAVE AN ONGOING CONVERSATION ABOUT EVERY ASPECT OF THEIR MARITAL RELATIONSHIP, INCLUDING SEX.**

wife said her husband was always working, and she was home with the kids all day, lonely and hurting. Then she met a guy who started taking her out to lunch, was good at listening, and showed an interest in her. They ended up in bed even though she was not really attracted to him and definitely didn't love him. With tears in his eyes, the husband explained there were sexual desires that were within the bounds of Scripture he'd always wanted to experience, but those things never happened in his marriage. At work, a woman brazenly approached him and asked him to do some of those very things, which they did after his impulsive and sinful decision. We asked him, "Would you have liked to meet your wife for lunch regularly, listen to her, give her some adult conversation, and be emotionally present?" He smiled and through his tears said, "I would love that, but you never said anything." She then interrupted him, saying, "I think it would be fun to try those things together, and I would have been happy to, but you never said anything."

I (Mark) looked at them both and said, "You could have had a conversation that led to a regular lunch together and fun time at a hotel as a married couple, but instead you both committed adultery." They both started weeping as this sober reality hit them. Had they simply had an ongoing conversation about their marriage and how to serve one another, their story would have been completely different. Thankfully, they repented of their sins, forgave one another, and put the work in to heal their marriage. Since then, they have been open and honest while sharing their testimony to encourage other couples to have open and honest discussions to avoid the disasters that happened because of their adulterous dalliances. The enemy knows our weaknesses and wants to divide our marriages so we will live silent and eventually separate lives. We need to be intentional about having conversations and learn to understand each other so we can better serve and enjoy each other!

Abbi closes this scene by speaking of those things she places in the reject category, urging her single friends not to cross God-given lines for sexual intimacy prior to marriage. Often, single people ask, "Where is the line?" when they should be asking, "When is the time?" The time for sexual intimacy is in marriage. Thus far as we have looked at various snapshots of the couple's relationship in the Song of Songs, it is possible they have kissed during their engagement, but they did not have sexual contact prior to marriage. Then they fully enjoy their freedoms in marriage. This theme of chastity before marriage and fidelity within marriage continues into the New Testament where we learn there should not even be a hint of sexual immorality among God's people,[11] there should be no sexual touch outside of marriage,[12] and Christian men are to treat Christian women as sisters.[13]

> **OFTEN, SINGLE PEOPLE ASK, "WHERE IS THE LINE?" WHEN THEY SHOULD BE ASKING, "WHEN IS THE TIME?"**

The sociological evidence only confirms the wisdom of God's Word. Women who cohabitate are more likely to be physically and sexually abused and even killed compared to a wife living with her husband.[xiii] Furthermore, those who cohabitate actually have higher divorce rates than couples who do not.[xiv] You can no more practice for being in covenant with someone

---

11 Ephesians 5:3

12 1 Corinthians 7:1

13 1 Timothy 5:1–2

than you can practice being in covenant with God—you are either in or out. The point is simple: God's way is the best way, and if there is sin in your past, then repent of it, heal up from it, and walk the path God created, which is frank and free heterosexual marriage. To help you enjoy the fullness of all God has for your marriage, the following discussion will be helpful if you begin with some time together, holding hands in prayer and inviting God the Holy Spirit to lead the conversation.

FACE-TO-FACE QUESTIONS
for Couple Discussion

1. What people are in your relationship who should not be? How can you draw boundaries with those people?

2. What people should be in your relationship to provide wise counsel? How can you invite those people in?

3. What good nicknames do you have for one another? Are there any bad nicknames you should never say again?

4. What does En Gedi look like in your home and on vacation?

5. What are some of the most enjoyable and unforgettable sexual memories you have together?

6. What are some new sexual things you would like to try in your marriage?

7. Is there any sexual sin in your past or present that you need to repent of and heal up from to fully enjoy married life as God intends? Is it time to bring in a professional like a Christian counselor to help you heal from past trauma or hurt so you are free in your marriage?

Chapter 3

THE LITTLE FOXES
2:8–3:5

She

2:8 Listen! My beloved!
Look! Here he comes,
leaping across the mountains,
bounding over the hills.

9 My beloved is like a gazelle or a young stag.
Look! There he stands behind our wall,
gazing through the windows,
peering through the lattice.

10 My beloved spoke and said to me,
"Arise, my darling,
my beautiful one, come with me.

11 See! The winter is past;
the rains are over and gone.

12 Flowers appear on the earth;
the season of singing has come,
the cooing of doves
is heard in our land.

13 The fig tree forms its early fruit;
the blossoming vines spread their fragrance.
Arise, come, my darling;
my beautiful one, come with me.

He

14 My dove in the clefts of the rock,
in the hiding places on the mountainside,
show me your face,
let me hear your voice;
for your voice is sweet,
and your face is lovely.

15 Catch for us the foxes,
the little foxes
that ruin the vineyards,
our vineyards that are in bloom.

She

16 My beloved is mine and I am his;
he browses among the lilies.

17 Until the day breaks
and the shadows flee,
turn, my beloved,
and be like a gazelle
or like a young stag
on the rugged hills.

3:1 All night long on my bed
I looked for the one my heart loves;
I looked for him but did not find him.

2 I will get up now and go about the city,
through its streets and squares;
I will search for the one my heart loves.
So I looked for him but did not find him.

3 The watchmen found me
as they made their rounds in the city.
"Have you seen the one my heart loves?"
4 Scarcely had I passed them
when I found the one my heart loves.
I held him and would not let him go
till I had brought him to my mother's house,
to the room of the one who conceived me.
5 Daughters of Jerusalem, I charge you
by the gazelles and by the does of the field:
Do not arouse or awaken love
until it so desires.

———————

When we started dating in the late 80s, there was a popular dance song called "Opposites Attract" by Paula Abdul. If you are not familiar with the song, then don't feel the urge to find it online, because your life will continue simply fine without it. Anyway, the gist of the playful love song is that a woman and her man are different in almost every way, and that's a good thing once they accept that their differences are their strength.

We are very different in every way except one. Whenever we take various marriage inventories, we score pretty much in complete agreement on our beliefs about our faith. On everything else, we are quite different.

- Mark likes to arrive everywhere early; Grace tends to be late.
- Mark prefers big potato chips; Grace likes the smaller crumbs.
- Mark is an introvert; Grace is an extrovert.
- Mark likes football; Grace really dislikes football.

- Mark is organized; Grace is more random.
- Mark is more of a pessimist; Grace is more of an optimist.
- Mark is impatient; Grace is patient.
- Mark likes to study with music cranked up; Grace prefers silence.
- Mark loves driving with the windows down; Grace does not.
- Mark doesn't get nervous when speaking in public; Grace does.
- Mark thinks writing a book about sex is fun; Grace ... not so much.

What about you and your spouse? In what ways are you opposite, and why do those differences that once attracted you to one another often annoy you now?

During the first days of a romantic relationship, we tend to be on our best behavior. We get dressed up, make sure our breath does not smell like Satan's gym shoes, and try our best to hide our quirks, eccentricities, and personal peculiarities in everything from how we drive our cars to how we chew our food and sneeze. We also hold all our intestinal gas in until we are married, and then many of us make up for lost time. When our variances do surface, they are quickly dismissed as interesting differences, which explains why the spender marries the saver, the night owl marries the early bird, the introvert ends up with the extrovert, the neatnik ends up with the slob, and the person who leaves the toilet seat down cannot live without the person who leaves it up. In essence, we overlook frustrations that will one day cut into our romance.

Many of our differences in marriage have nothing to do with sin. Often, our spouses are not violating any of God's laws, but they are violating one of our rules. We've all got our own ways of doing things and tend to think that our way is the right way.

Then, we really get to know one another, especially after we've been married a while. Eventually, we've not only prayed over one another but also found innumerable ways to annoy one another.

I (Grace) am easily annoyed when Mark doesn't load the dishwasher correctly, wants to watch certain boring TV shows, and adds a topping or ingredient when dinner is already served. None of those things are sin, but if I stew about them and let my heart grumble, then it starts to tear down our marriage and romance. I can either talk to Mark about them and ask him to be aware, or I can let them go and recognize I also create annoyances.

I (Mark) do not understand why you need to clean the dishes before you put them in the dishwasher—it only has one job and should not delegate that job to me. I find guys building houses and cars as the last hope for a world filled with beta-males, and I do not understand anything about cooking because I have been spoiled by my wife for our entire marriage and have the spiritual gift of going out to dinner.

How about you and your spouse? What are the things that annoy you about one another, cause ongoing frustrations, and feel like a stubbed toe that keeps getting bumped?

The Two Train Tracks of Life

A wise pastor once said that he used to see life as good seasons and bad seasons, with the goal being to push through the bad seasons to get to the good seasons. Then, he learned over time that life is like two train tracks running side by side throughout life. One track is good things that we are enjoy-ing or looking forward to. The other track is bad things that we're suffering through or not looking forward to. Every day, life travels on both tracks at the same time. In our marriage, I (Mark), in homage to my initials M.A.D. (Mark Alan Driscoll) more easily act like the pessimist and notice the bad track, whereas Grace, true to her name, is more of an optimist and focuses on the good track.

The analogy of two tracks is entirely true, nowhere more so than in our romantic relationships. In this section of the Song of Songs, we see the two tracks in full view as the couple starts with flirting and ends with fighting.

When Abbi is "gazing through the windows, peering through the lattice" (2:9), it does not mean she's stalking Solomon; rather, she's anxiously awaiting her beloved to come to her parent's house where she is living prior to their marriage to head out on a fun, romantic date together. Solomon arrives and invites her to "arise, my darling, my beautiful one, come with me" (2:10). In this scene, we witness the power of the ministry of presence. One of the great blessings of marriage is the ministry of presence with our spouse. When God said it was not good to be alone, His solution for that problem was a spouse. The reason Abbi is waiting eagerly and looking intently is because every moment with someone you love is sacred. How wonderful is it that God did not just speak to us from heaven, but He also came down to be present with us in Jesus Christ. Jesus knew we would fear abandonment when He ascended back into heaven, so He told us in John's Gospel that when He went up, the Holy Spirit would come down. God's ministry of

EVERY MOMENT WITH SOMEONE YOU LOVE IS SACRED.

presence would always be with us and, in fact, *in* us as believers in Jesus Christ. The ministry of presence cannot be overstated. Being together is a blessing and explains why a healthy married couple cannot wait to get home from work, looks forward to weekends off and vacations away, and waits at the airport when a dad returns from a long military deployment, running to enjoy the ministry of presence.

Their date opens by Abbi passionately flirting with her man. She calls Solomon her young stud or stag, something that men still like to hear some 3,000 years later. In saying that winter is over, spring has come, and their love is in full bloom, the comparison is between the season they are in annually and the season they are in romantically. Curiously, springtime seems to be the time for love. Most weddings are in the spring, and we had our first date in the spring (March 12, 1988, to be exact).

It is important for married couples to be aware of seasons. Life goes through them, and a couple needs to be aware of the change in seasons and determine how they can best love and serve one another when a new one comes along while continuing to their marriage. When a couple is dating, their lives are still somewhat independent. Once they marry, they must figure out how to live as one, with one schedule and one budget, which takes some intentional effort. Adding children changes literally everything and requires an incredible amount of physical effort from both mom and dad. As the kids get older, they have more activities and friends along with school, so the husband and wife need to orient a lot of their time and energy around the growing needs of their children. In the teen years, a lot of discipleship is done regarding everything from having your own faith, managing money, choosing friends, navigating romantic relationships, learning to drive, planning for post-high school life, and choosing career paths. The college years are expensive and require a lot of coaching. Once a child moves out on their own, there is still a lot of energy invested in helping the child launch as an independent adult. The empty nest years require a couple to reset their entire life together, make sure their marriage is a priority, help their adult children get married and start their own families, and look after aging parents. Eventually, the couple ages and deals with their own health and career issues, along with welcoming grandchildren. Every season of life has opportunities to build and obstacles to break a marriage. Understanding the season you are in helps make the most of every one of them. When a couple fails to recognize they have entered a new season, they tend to be stuck in how they previously operated, which no longer works and causes pains and problems.

> **WHEN A COUPLE FAILS TO RECOGNIZE THEY HAVE ENTERED A NEW SEASON, THEY TEND TO BE STUCK IN HOW THEY PREVIOUSLY OPERATED, WHICH NO LONGER WORKS AND CAUSES PAINS AND PROBLEMS.**

If you've ever seen a couple so dripping with love and oozing adoration for each other to the degree that they are a little awkward to be around, then you get the sense of what Abbi is saying. Solomon flirtatiously responds by calling her "darling," "my beautiful one," and "my dove." For the ancient Hebrews, the dove was considered ceremonially clean and an acceptable sacrifice that was pleasing to God; it was even offered by Jesus' parents at the Temple.[14] The dove is also a symbol of purity[15] and later a symbol of the Holy Spirit.[16] He then reminds her how much he loves the look of her face and sound of her voice.

At this point, things are headed in a romantic dalliance direction, quickly moving toward some terrific times. One observation from their interactions is that most women tend to be more verbal, and most men are more visual. Abbi has a lot to say here and throughout the Song of Songs. Remember, in the Song of Songs, she speaks firstly, freely, and frankly. A lot of what she expresses is emotional—how she is feeling and what she is desiring. Like most men, Solomon uses less words and speaks about what he enjoys seeing—in this scene, her face and eyes.

From Flirting to Fighting

Like a perfectly cooked meal that gets dropped on the floor before a bite is taken, everything goes bad very quickly. We've all had this same experience—the day or the date starts good but ends bad. Like a car wreck we did not see coming, we are blindsided and dumbfounded that a good start had a sudden bad ending with the air bags deployed and a lot of confusion. Why does this happen? The answer is "little foxes that ruin the vineyards" (2:15).

A vineyard could take years or even generations to nurture. The constant watering, pruning, and cultivating was an art form that produced grapes for wine. Some years ago, we toured a winery in Sonoma, California, that was owned by a

---

14 Luke 2:22–28

15 Psalm 68:13

16 Matthew 3:16

Christian family. If you were raised in a strict Christian home that forbid alcohol, please remember our trip was entirely devoted to Bible study and learning about the numerous viti-cultural metaphors, and when we drank the wine, we did so solely for research purposes in a King James Bible. Anyway, as we toured their large family vineyard, the owners reminded us of all the times the Bible uses the imagery of a vine, branches, fruit, and harvest. As we stopped at one dying vine, they told us the meaning of this image in Song of Songs. Apparently, a small animal had gotten into the vineyard and gnawed at the base of an old and prized vine, which caused it to begin dying. The point of this Scripture is little things can get into the vineyard of a marriage and gnaw away at the root of our vine, causing our love to start to wither and die.

A fox in your vineyard is any little thing that gnaws away at your enjoyment and love for one another. Examples of foxes in the vineyard includes a poorly architected marriage where the priorities of God, spouse, kids, work, and *then* extended family are out of order. The intrusion of extended family or friends who do not respect healthy boundaries is another common fox in the vineyard. Another would be simple disorganization where the schedule, chores, and budget are a mess and sources of constant frustration. Pain from past hurts that remain unforgiven or unhealed can also be a fox in your vineyard. Some seasons are simply tough, like when one of you has bad health, a child is born, older parents are sickly, or you just cannot come to an agreement on a critical issue

> **A FOX IN YOUR VINEYARD IS ANY LITTLE THING THAT GNAWS AWAY AT YOUR ENJOYMENT AND LOVE FOR ONE ANOTHER.**

and need to go to counseling for help. Financial pressure, job loss, unexpected medical bills, and other mounting cash crises are common foxes that gnaw away at the vine of a marriage. Shame over secret past or present sin, such as pornography, is a common fox in the vineyard. Annoyances also count, as it's not always sins but simply differences that can gnaw away at a marriage. These can include answering the phone during dinner, not going to bed at the same time, not helping with household chores, or disagreeing about how to parent the children. Snoring loudly, belching frequently, spending frivolously, and freaking out frequently are also good candidates to qualify as foxes in your vineyard.

One common fox in the vineyard is differing visions for the home that lead to repeated conflict. Most people would never live in a home that did not have an architect who designed it and a builder who constructed it. However, most people build lives that they have not intentionally architected.

There are several similar versions of a story in which a large boat was tied to a dock and two men walked up to survey it. One man asked the other, "In regard to that boat, who is the most important person?" Without a pause, the answer was, "The captain." The man who asked the question then responded, "Incorrect. The most important person is the boat builder. The best captain in the world cannot succeed with a boat that does not float." This analogy holds true for many areas of our lives but especially in our marriages. Too often a husband and wife are so busy working that they do not take the time to step back and work on their lives. The result is lots of foxes in the vineyard.

In college, we had a professor share with us the three common types of households:

1. Random Homes: There is little order, structure, scheduling, or planning. People eat meals whenever they want, rather than sitting down together. Bedtimes are chaotic and sporadic, and sometimes there are not even assigned beds for the children because they simply crash wherever they choose every night. Guests come and go out of the house as they please, and curfews and chores are nonexistent.

2. Closed Homes: There is much order, structure, scheduling, and planning. The family sits down at a regular time for dinner, weeks are scheduled and organized, the home has systems and chores to keep it tidy, bedtime is consistent, and people cannot simply drop by the home unannounced. Instead, they need to schedule an agreed upon time in advance.

3. Open Homes: These are somewhere between Random Homes and Open Homes. There is more order, structure, scheduling, and planning than a Random Home but not as much as a Closed Home. Most of the time, the family sits down for dinner but not always. Approved friends and extended family members are welcome to drop by unannounced, but everyone else needs to ask in advance.[xv]

I (Grace) grew up in a home with one parent who wanted an Open home and the other wanted a Closed home. It led to confusion and frustration in the marriage and with the kids, as we weren't sure what was expected at any given time. Sadly, it also made manipulation of my parents far too common since they didn't agree. We had uninvited people constantly showing up for dinner, random stray animals that would be adopted, the same chores our entire childhood, semi-consistent bedtimes, and a general curfew that was often broken. My parents went above and beyond to serve the people in the church that they pastored.

I (Mark) grew up in a home that was more Open to Random. I had one of the only dads in my neighborhood, and my mom stayed home to raise five kids, of whom I was the oldest. Since most of the kids in our neighborhood had a mom who was at work as their only parent, they ended up at our house a lot. My parents were gracious to clothe, feed, and provide a safe place for the kids in our neighborhood. As a result, we had an intact family that sat down for meals and had bedtime and structure, but we also had random kids showing up at random times with random needs. To this day, I am really proud of how my parents opened their lives and home to help kids stay out of trouble and have a warm meal, safe place to sleep, and even a coat or shoes if they did not have those basic provisions. My dad even built a batting cage in the backyard and bought a pitching machine to give the neighborhood boys something to do other than sin and folly.

Early in our marriage, Grace and I led a college ministry and hosted Bible studies multiple nights a week in our home. Eventually, this morphed into a church plant, and we started adding our eventual five children every other year. Our struggling church consisted mainly of broke college kids, so the interns, Bible studies, and counseling sessions, along with the church offices and study, were all contained in our home. I am a strong introvert, so I was losing my mind as people constantly came and went through our house. In one year, we had a few thousand people in our home, and I taught everyone the Bible while Grace fed them. We had a Random Home, and I wanted to transition to a Closed Home to get our life and family boundaries back. Because we did not agree on the big picture of how we were going to manage our home, we ended up having conflicts over all kinds of small things and individual relationships. Almost everyone and everything became a fox in our vineyard. After many conversations, we agreed that for the safety and health of our family and, as we've had seasons of genuine threat and attack, we needed a home that was somewhere between Closed and Open, depending upon what season we were in.

Today, technology keeps trying to turn every house into a Random Home. Our phones demands that we pay more attention to them than our spouses or even our God. In days past, people would have to get in a car and travel to someone's house, hoping they were home, to barge into their marriage and family. Today, almost everyone you know can do that whenever they want for whatever they want. The constant distraction and disruption of technology leads to much division and damage in a marriage. In our constantly connected and chaotic world, we need to learn how to manage the people we interact with not just physically but also digitally. Social media can never replace our spouses, and if we live on our phones, constantly available to anyone trying to communicate with us, then the least healthy people will surely take the best of our time and energy, which should belong to our relationship with God and then our spouses as our first priorities. Setting boundaries with technology and people will help safeguard your marriage. The phone (and other technology) is likely the fox that moved into the vineyard of most marriages and is busy gnawing away at any and every fruitful vine.

Every marriage has had foxes in the vineyard, and they may still be there. As we mentioned before, I (Grace) lean more toward extroversion and can feel energized by being with people. Mark, on the other hand, loves people but is extremely drained after socializing. This was a fox in our vineyard (and still can be) because I thought it was a sin that Mark needed to repent for rather than the way God created him so he can more effectively and passionately focus on preaching the Bible. Meanwhile, Mark thought my regular time with people was me neglecting my priorities. This issue ate away at our marriage until we were able to see that we could find ways to serve each other better by being gracious with personality differences, while also challenging each other to grow and not let our personalities give us excuses. I needed to pull back from having people over to our house constantly and look through the calendar to see when he had the most energy to give to house guests. Mark needed to be open to spontaneous social times when we couldn't schedule them. I also make sure I am prioritizing my time with him so he knows our marriage matters to me rather than spending constant time with other ladies and giving him the leftovers. If we had let this go and not talked about it, then resentment and bitterness would have eaten away at both of us and ultimately wrecked our marriage. When left untended, issues big and small will cause destruction in the relationship and erase romantic pursuit.

I (Mark) needed to realize that Grace has the spiritual gift of hospitality. She enjoys having people over, feeding them, and caring for them. The problem was that when we had people over, it was a workday for me as a pastor because people would want to talk about theology or counseling issues in our home, and I wanted to save my home as a place to get a break from pastoring people. I also really appreciated all the ways Grace tirelessly served me and our kids. Honestly, we are all very spoiled by her, and I selfishly did not want to share her with others. Meanwhile, she was at home all day with little kids and just wanted to have some adult conversations, fun parties, and events. We learned, through repeatedly failing, to get time with people on our calendar so I could prepare for the emotional output, and Grace got more organized with our social life so we had a healthy rhythm with friends and extended family that we both enjoyed.

What are the foxes in your vineyard?

The Four Horsemen of Marriage Apocalypse

When a fox shows up in your vineyard, how each member of the couple responds is crucial. In this scene in the Song of Songs, the couple says a fox got in their vineyard, and they don't tell exactly what it was. Nonetheless, they did not deal with it well, and it led to a heated conflict in which Solomon walked out, and Abbi had no idea where he had gone.

When foxes show up in our vineyards, bad conflict resolution patterns emerge, adding even more foxes. Marriage expert John Gottman, whose method predicts divorce probability with a 91 percent accuracy,[xvi] identifies what he calls "the four horsemen" of marriage apocalypse. Marriage dissolution begins with a "harsh startup"[xvii] (criticism or sarcasm), which only becomes more extreme and descends into the following pattern, pulling hell up into the marriage instead of inviting heaven down into it:

1. **Criticism:** Unlike a concern or a complaint about an issue, this response is very personal so that the other person does not just have a problem but also *is* the problem.

2. **Contempt:** Sneering, mocking, name calling, eye rolling, and volume raising communicate personal disgust and disdain for the other person as the goal becomes winning instead of worshipping.

3. **Defensiveness**: Rather than repenting of how we are treating the other person, we make excuses and blame shift so that it's their fault, all to double down on the fight or attempt to change the subject if we sense we are losing the battle.

4. **Stonewalling**: We tune out, practice the silent treatment, leave the room, drive away, or otherwise disengage so that what was a heated battle now becomes a cold war. Generally, it is the husband who chooses this lonely path of ignoring one another, and that is exactly what we see in the marital battle in the Song of Songs.[xviii]

Often, big fights occur in our romantic relationships over petty things. Why does this happen? While the issue may not be a big deal, the person responsible for it is. This fact explains why a stranger or an enemy can do something that is bad and big without much effect to our emotional well-being for months and years afterward. Conversely, a person near and dear to us can do something comparatively minor, and it sends us into a tailspin because we have higher expectations when we have opened our hearts to them in ways that cause their sins or failures to be more painful.

During one counseling session with an older couple, the wife lamented that for years of their marriage, her husband had an ongoing habit of saying, "That was a fail" whenever she made a mistake. It did not occur often, but it was often enough to discourage her. If she dropped dinner on the floor, got a dent on her car door, or showed up late because she lost track of time, he would say, "That was a fail." She already felt bad and knew she had failed, but he added to the situation. As she explained how this habit hurt her, her husband shrugged it off by saying, "It's not a big deal." She then responded, "You are a big deal to me. What you say may not be a big deal, but I love you, and when you say that, it hurts me because you are a big deal to me." After years of ignoring her pleas, he finally understood that it's not just *what* is said, but also *who* says it that determines what is and is not a big deal.

Additionally, we spend so much time with our spouses that quirky little habits become patterns that drive us nuttier than a peanut factory because of their regularity. This reality explains why some couples have more conflict the more time they spend together. Vacations and holidays are prime times for marital conflicts to escalate easily. The home lockdown as a response to COVID-19, for example, caused many couples to get on one another's nerves like never before and set divorces in motion. In this section of the Song of Songs, this is what happens. A fox got in their vineyard, which explains why Abbi closes this section of Scripture by talking about how they were separated, Solomon left, and she could not find him, which only added to her distress.

Make the First Move

In some ways, the relationship between North and South Korea is like a dysfunctional marriage. The two sides tried for years to get along but to no avail. Eventually, a demilitarized zone was built to ensure each side kept to themselves, and they never interacted. They do not have any contact, because if they did, a war would erupt.

In marriage, stonewalling left over time can lead to a similar relationship. The Bible opens with God creating marriage and telling us in Genesis 2:24 that we need to "cleave," "be joined," "become united," "stick with," "hold fast," or "cling to," depending on which English translation of the Bible you read. The big idea is we should continually and passionately pursue our spouses so that we can live together, united as "one." The opposite occurs in stonewalling, as we lose our passion for our spouse and do not pursue them. Often, the opposite of love is not hate but indifference. We become two people living separate lives with the equivalent of a demilitarized zone to keep us from interacting out of fear of yet another war breaking out.

> **OFTEN, THE OPPOSITE OF LOVE IS NOT HATE BUT INDIFFERENCE.**

Examples of stonewalling include:

- not coming home
- sleeping in different beds
- keeping different schedules
- spending time in different parts of the home to avoid one another
- communicating through the children or technology rather than face to face
- the husband retreating to the garage or man cave
- the wife retreating to the kitchen or laundry room
- one or both spending lots of time away working, hanging out with friends, or enjoying hobbies

Obviously, these activities are not harmful in small doses, but if they are done simply to avoid a spouse, then they can be deadly to a marriage. In extreme cases, a couple will remain legally married but functionally divorced, possibly even living and working in different cities, not because they have to but because they choose that way of life to avoid each other.

If we're honest, every couple has seasons in which a fox gets in the vineyard, a good day goes bad, and stonewalling occurs. The longer this behavior goes on, the greater the opportunity Satan has to infect your vineyard with bitterness and selfishness. He will use this silence as an opportunity to whisper in your ears, setting a negative narrative about your spouse that becomes a lens by which you view them as the problem. We can never forget that Satan did not even show up until Adam and Eve were married, as after the wedding comes the war. Our first parents started well, but then things went bad as they stonewalled and separated. Thankfully, the Lord came looking for them, just as He does for every believing couple ever since. Once the Lord has dealt with our anger, hurt, bitterness, and selfishness, He wants us to go searching for our spouse to treat them as He has treated us.

In this scene from the Song of Songs, Solomon is the one stonewalling, and Abbi is the one searching. Unless one pursues the other, they will no longer enjoy the principle of mutual belonging that she rejoiced over when she said, "My beloved is mine and I am his."[17] Unless one pursues the other, they will never get back to "we" because they will be both stuck in "me." The difference between *we* and *me* is the difference between warm unity and cold division.

The key to any healthy, holy, and happy marriage is for both the husband and the wife to be givers and forgivers. Our God is a giver and forgiver, and we must follow His example if we are going to have a godly marriage He will bless. Whenever the marriage has one person who gives and one who takes,

---

17 2:16

> ## "THE DIFFERENCE BETWEEN *WE* AND *ME* IS THE DIFFERENCE BETWEEN WARM UNITY AND COLD DIVISION."

it is an abusive relationship. If only one person is pursuing, praying, forgiving, and serving, then it is more of a master-to-slave relationship than it is a husband-to-wife covenant. The principle of mutual belonging means both the husband and wife give all that they have and are to one another.

In this scene Abbi needs to give, and Solomon needs to forgive. So she pursues him to apologize and mend the broken fence that let the fox into their vineyard. He forgives her, and they work things out.

Eventually Abbi finds Solomon and brings him back to her parents' home. Their romantic relationship started by him visiting her there, so she takes him back to where they fell in love to remind them both of why they are together in the first place. She concludes by reminding her unmarried friends not to arouse or awaken the sexual aspect of a relationship until the right time, which is a wise admonition. Sometimes a couple who is not yet married but is fighting ends up in bed together as the emotions are running high, and the desire to connect is particularly strong when the relationship is strained and in the process of reconciling. When we are single and a fox shows up in our vineyard, sleeping together to feel close and connected is just adding a bigger fox to the vineyard as we are not solving our problems but rather multiplying them.

Fight For Your Marriage, Not with Your Spouse

In closing, what we witness throughout the Song of Songs is both the husband and wife are strong personalities. He is the King of Israel, and no one would ever dream of telling him what to do, rebuking him, doing most of the talking in his presence, or acting like a peer. His beloved, however, does those very things. Abbi is an incredibly strong person, the kind of wife he needs to have a healthy, loving marriage.

The truth is, we are both extraordinarily strong personalities with strong opinions. We have found that in marriage, strength is not a problem. Independence, however, is always a problem. When we operate independently of our spouse or, even worse, independently of our God, nothing good happens. This truth can be seen all the way back to the Garden where our first parents ruined their marriage and our human family by acting independently from God and one another, which is the cause for sin.

In this scene of the Song of Songs, we see that Solomon and Abbi are both acting independently. What started as flirting and time together ends with fighting and time apart. The key to a strong marriage is working with our God and spouse, especially when foxes show up in our marriage vineyard, to serve and forgive one another.

It might seem odd that a book of the Bible devoted entirely to the passions and pleasures of marriage reports not only flirting but also the pain of fighting. However, the Bible is the

> **WE HAVE FOUND THAT IN MARRIAGE, STRENGTH IS NOT A PROBLEM. INDEPENDENCE, HOWEVER, IS ALWAYS A PROBLEM.**

most honest book ever written, and every honest couple knows they are going to have some fights. The key is to learn how to fight for your marriage, rather than fighting with your spouse. To help you do that very thing, we have an exercise for you to do together that will help you avoid a harsh startup if you have "foxes in your vineyard" to discuss. The key is to begin with a lengthy time in prayer, inviting the Lord into the conversation so that you are both dependent on the Holy Spirit.

FACE-TO-FACE QUESTIONS
for Couple Discussion

1. What are the good and bad things in your marriage and life right now, running like parallel train tracks? On which track are you most likely to focus?

2. Lovingly, kindly, and patiently discuss some of the foxes in your vineyard to which you both need to pay attention. What will happen if they are not kept from gnawing away at your relationship?

3. What are some bad patterns you can honestly and humbly own that you fall into when the two of you have an argument or disagreement? How can you repent of those, and what can you do differently as you go forward?

4. What unhealthy habits did you establish before you were married that you need to be aware of because they are negatively affecting your marriage now (e.g., the four ways a disagreement goes deadly as listed in this chapter, or sexual sin together so that the relationship was not built upon the worship of God and holy friendship but rather sexual pleasure)?

Chapter 4

HIS GARDEN
3:6 — 5:1

She

3:6 Who is this coming up from the wilderness
like a column of smoke,
perfumed with myrrh and incense
made from all the spices of the merchant?

7 Look! It is Solomon's carriage,
escorted by sixty warriors,
the noblest of Israel,

8 all of them wearing the sword,
all experienced in battle,
each with his sword at his side,
prepared for the terrors of the night.

9 King Solomon made for himself the carriage;
he made it of wood from Lebanon.

10 Its posts he made of silver,
its base of gold.
Its seat was upholstered with purple,
its interior inlaid with love.

Daughters of Jerusalem,
11 come out, and look, you daughters of Zion.
Look on King Solomon wearing a crown,
the crown with which his mother crowned him
on the day of his wedding,
the day his heart rejoiced.

He

4:1 How beautiful you are, my darling!
Oh, how beautiful!
Your eyes behind your veil are doves.
Your hair is like a flock of goats
descending from the hills of Gilead.
2 Your teeth are like a flock of sheep just shorn,
coming up from the washing.
Each has its twin;
not one of them is alone.
3 Your lips are like a scarlet ribbon;
your mouth is lovely.
Your temples behind your veil
are like the halves of a pomegranate.
4 Your neck is like the tower of David,
built with courses of stone;
on it hang a thousand shields,
all of them shields of warriors.
5 Your breasts are like two fawns,
like twin fawns of a gazelle
that browse among the lilies.
6 Until the day breaks
And the shadows flee,
I will go to the mountain of myrrh
and to the hill of incense.
7 You are altogether beautiful, my darling;

there is no flaw in you.

8 Come with me from Lebanon, my bride,
come with me from Lebanon.
Descend from the crest of Amana,
from the top of Senir, the summit of Hermon,
from the lions' dens
and the mountain haunts of leopards.

9 You have stolen my heart, my sister, my bride;
you have stolen my heart
with one glance of your eyes,
with one jewel of your necklace.

10 How delightful is your love, my sister, my bride!
How much more pleasing is your love than wine,
and the fragrance of your perfume
more than any spice!

11 Your lips drop sweetness as the honeycomb, my bride;
milk and honey are under your tongue.
The fragrance of your garments
is like the fragrance of Lebanon.

12 You are a garden locked up, my sister, my bride;
you are a spring enclosed, a sealed fountain.

13 Your plants are an orchard of pomegranates
with choice fruits,
with henna and nard,

14 nard and saffron,
calamus and cinnamon,
with every kind of incense tree,
with myrrh and aloes
and all the finest spices.

15 You are a garden fountain,
a well of flowing water
streaming down from Lebanon.

She

> **16** Awake, north wind,
> and come, south wind!
> Blow on my garden,
> that its fragrance may spread everywhere.
> Let my beloved come into his garden
> and taste its choice fruits.

He

> **5:1** I have come into my garden, my sister, my bride;
> I have gathered my myrrh with my spice.
> I have eaten my honeycomb and my honey;
> I have drunk my wine and my milk.

Friends

> Eat, friends, and drink;
> drink your fill of love.

―――――――

Throughout life, we often take photos of the most important and memorable moments. There is one day, however, that we spend a lot of money to hire a professional photographer to take our most important pictures—our wedding day!

If it's been a while since you have looked at your wedding photos, then it's a good idea to revisit them now and then, remember why you fell in love, and rekindle any passion that's been waning. When our kids were young, we left our wedding photo album out where they could flip through the pages with us as we explained how we met, our favorite dating times together, our wedding day, honeymoon, and life together before their arrival.

We were 21 years old, between our junior and senior years of college. We worked a lot of hours all summer to save as much money as we could, knowing we would spend our first year of marriage going to school full-time and working part-time. We were married in August on an unusually sweltering day and had two pastors preach (our college pastor who did our premarital counseling and Grace's dad). We had a large wedding with hundreds and hundreds of people as well as seven bridesmaids and seven groomsmen. The church we were married in had no air conditioning, so it was an uncomfortable day in dresses and tuxes. We were completely emotionally and physically worn out from both working two jobs all summer and welcoming all our wedding guests. For our honeymoon, we drove to the Oregon Coast for a few days, and we were so tired that we did not wake up the next day until 4 pm, just in time to eat dinner.

The two most important decisions anyone makes is who will be their God and who will be their spouse. Those are the only two covenant relationships, which is why getting married as a believer with God present is a sacred moment on a special day. We were young, broke, exhausted, in love, and happy to be able to do life together every day and enjoy the simple things.

> **THE TWO MOST IMPORTANT DECISIONS ANYONE MAKES IS WHO WILL BE THEIR GOD AND WHO WILL BE THEIR SPOUSE.**

Most women start planning their weddings when they are little girls and even dress up to practice for it. Planning a wedding is a big deal, much bigger than most men could even imagine until they are part of the process. Now, imagine an ancient wedding in the near east that would last up to a week with the marriage consummated on the first night, followed by days of feasting, ceremony, and celebration. Jesus' first miracle was turning water into wine at a wedding in Cana of Galilee to spare the family the shame of running out of supplies. Throughout Jesus' ministry, parties of various sorts were snapshots of what life will be like in God's Kingdom. At Trinity Church, which we planted in the Arizona desert, we like to say we throw epic, fun parties to practice for heaven since parties are the places Jesus showed up to help people practice for heaven.

Add to it the royal wedding of King Solomon, and the pageantry and security had to be completely over the top, which Abbi explains. In this section, the couple arrives at their wedding day and the consummation of their marriage covenant.

What was your wedding day like? What was your honeymoon night like? What are your favorite memories from that sacred day you entered your marriage covenant and consummated it?

Putting the Fun into Marriage Fundamentals

Returning to the story of the Song of Songs, as the couple approached their wedding day, they had numerous frank and private conversations about their wedding night and life together. They have been honest about their fears and their hopes. Now, the time has come for them to begin their new life as "one" as God intended.

We again see two things in their interaction that are generally true of most men and women. Admittedly, some women are more visual, and some men are more verbal but, as a general rule, the opposite is most often true. Men tend to be visual. Women tend to be verbal.

First, throughout Song of Songs, including this section, Abbi is very verbal. Once again, she speaks first and has a lot to say in this section as well as throughout the book. Looking in the distance, eager for his arrival, she notes that her soon-to-be husband is arriving in a custom-made chariot constructed with special timber from the woods of Lebanon along with gold, silver, and purple fabric, which was the most rare and expensive color dye in the ancient world. This is an over-the-top princess wedding that all her girlfriends would be stunned by and speaking about for years to come.

Accompanying Solomon are 60 special forces soldiers ready for battle. As a man should, he takes every effort to ensure Abbi's safety. In his example, we see that one of the duties of a husband is to be mindful and active for the safety of his wife. In our marriage, this includes me always buying Grace a large, heavy SUV to drive around with the kids and living in safe neighborhoods with security systems on our homes. In various seasons of ministry where we had real threats to our safety, this included taking additional safety measures at our home and church. As men, we generally do not feel unsafe, but in talking with Grace and other women, I learned they often do feel unsafe. As men, it is important to ask our wives how we can help create an environment in which they feel safe and cared for.

Second, throughout Song of Songs but especially in this section, Solomon is very visual. Since the wedding night is incredibly important for a healthy start to a couple's sex life, and Abbi has already expressed some insecurity about her appearance, he is very lavish with his encouragement and specific compliments of her long and dark hair, teeth, lips (good for French kissing long before the French), cheeks, long neck, and breasts. The mention of all the different scents is a reminder that women smell much different (and better) than men. You can tell whether a woman lives in a home by simply walking in and taking a whiff. If it smells like Satan's feet, then only single guys live there. If it smells like candles, potpourri, flowers, or perfume, then you know a female is involved. After spending years sharing a bedroom with brothers and showering in locker rooms with other guys after games, any sane man greatly appreciates the scent of his girlfriend or wife. When asked why he married his wife, one guy even told us, "She smelled like vanilla."

In saying Abbi's hair is "like a flock of goats" (4:1), Solomon is comparing her long, black hair flowing down her shoulders and onto her back to the beautiful scene of numerous goats on the lovely hills of Gilead with their lush black color shining in the sun. Gazing at her face, he also notes that her teeth are a brilliant white, and she has all of them, which was rare in an age with next to no dental care and probably means she did not play hockey. She has a long neck he finds very alluring, and she adorns it with jewels and metal jewelry. As an aside, many women do not have long necks, but it is a unique feature in Abbi's appearance that Solomon finds sexy. It just goes to show, sometimes the aspects of our appearance that we might be insecure about because they are distinct are the very things that our spouse finds alluring.

The meaning of "Your breasts are like two fawns, like twin fawns of a gazelle that browse among the lilies" (4:5) can easily be lost on modern readers. Most women would not be excited to have this part of their body referred to as a furry creature on their wedding night, but that's not the intended meaning. Solomon certainly is not talking about Moses and Aaron who fed God's people the pure milk of the Torah, which is the interpretation of the ancient Midrash Rabbah.

Neither is this in reference to the Old and New Testaments that provide the Church the pure milk of God's Word, as some early Christian commentators taught. Other peculiar interpretations include Psellus's teaching that this was the blood and water that flowed from the side of Christ on the cross or the twin spiritual disciplines of contemplation and action, as taught by Christian mystics. No, Solomon is looking forward to consummating his marriage with his wife. If you've ever seen newborn twin baby deer, then you know they tend to be very playful, cute, and found in the petting section of the zoo because it's fun to touch them. That's more precisely what is being said. Additionally, some Bible commentators think the mention of hills and mountains may be a clever way Solomon speaks of enjoying her breasts and various other curves.

The mention of mountain peaks is a way of inviting Abbi to climb from one height of passion to the next on their exciting and exhilarating lovemaking honeymoon adventure. Hikers will tell you that each peak of a climb has its own exciting experience to enjoy, and the same is true for lovers.

In calling her "my sister, my bride," Solomon is pointing to a particularly important marriage principle in the Bible. Before a woman is a man's bride, she is God's daughter and the man's spiritual sister. In 1 Timothy 5:2, Paul tells Timothy to treat "younger women as sisters, with absolute purity." A good marriage begins with a good friendship between two Christians who pray together, worship, learn from the Bible, and serve God in church. After your marriage, you remain brother and sister in Christ and add to that role the relationship of husband and wife. Worshipping and serving God has been at the bedrock of our marriage, and we would urge you to believe that this order of spiritual friendship first and marital relationship second is crucial. If you erred in the early years of your relationship by placing sex, hobbies, or something else as the foundation of your relationship, then it's not too late to lay a new foundation based upon your spiritual life together. We would encourage the husband to take initiative in spiritual things as the statistics reveal that it is usually the woman who is spiritually active and the husband who is inactive. If we learn anything from the story of Adam and Eve and the first marriage, it is that a passive man opens the door for Satan to be the head of his household.

In saying "There is no flaw in you" (4:7), Solomon is declaring that Abbi is his standard of beauty. He compares her to no one else, and she is completely adored and desired by her husband on their wedding night. This is a theme throughout their relationship and a good reminder to husbands that only having eyes for your wife and inviting her to see herself through your eyes is the only way to have a free and fun sex life.

> THIS IS A THEME THROUGHOUT THEIR RELATIONSHIP AND A GOOD REMINDER TO HUSBANDS THAT ONLY HAVING EYES FOR YOUR WIFE AND INVITING HER TO SEE HERSELF THROUGH YOUR EYES IS THE ONLY WAY TO HAVE A FREE AND FUN SEX LIFE.

He compares their wedding night to being welcomed into a private garden with amazing smells and flowing water. Unlike a public park that is open to anyone, Solomon had private renowned gardens that were kept for his enjoyment alone, and no one else could enter the king's sacred space. In the middle of ancient private gardens was a fountain with fresh water. He uses that beautiful, private, and poetic imagery to speak of the first night of sexual intimacy with his wife. Assured of Solomon's love, Abbi invites him to enjoy lovemaking together. One Bible commentator says, "The woman speaks here, inviting her beloved to come and share sexual intimacy with her."[xix] Another Bible commentator further explains that this might be a reference to her inviting oral sex and then consummation of their marriage: "She now invites him to come into the garden of her life in the fullest possible way. It may be locked to others, but it is certainly not locked to him. The phrase 'I could eat you' is not such a modern expression. Here she invites him to do that very thing."[xx]

To consummate their marriage, after a lot of flirting, Abbi invites Solomon to be with her, which is an important detail. This marriage, along with its sexual relationship, is not abusive, domineering, or forcible in any way. She welcomes her husband, and they have discussed in detail exactly what they want to do and have agreed on the bare details. Apparently, they took their time on their wedding night because the plan was to be sexually active all night, "until the day breaks and the shadows flee" (4:6). This is nakedness without shame as God intended.

Once their marriage covenant is consummated, their family and friends who are present as witnesses for the wedding celebrate this new family, now one flesh, in the sight of God and add their approval. The first day of their marriage is incredible.

If you are engaged to be married and reading this, you are looking forward to your wedding day and hoping that everything comes together flawlessly as it did for Solomon and Abbi. If you are married, this section of their story is a reminder to look back at all the work that went into your wedding day and celebrate this wonderful moment of God's grace in your life.

The Most Important Day of Your Marriage Is the Last Day

While the wedding day is important, it is not the *most* important day of your marriage. The most important day of your marriage is the last day, not the first day. Couples commonly invest an incredible amount of time, energy, and money into their first day. Detailed plans are made, and everything is purposefully organized. While this is great, it can be in vain unless you have the same commitment to planning the last day of your marriage.

Looking into the future, will your last day of marriage be followed by a divorce, or will you still be married? Will your last day of marriage be a lonely one filled with remorse and regret or a lovely one filled with rejoicing and remembering?

Tragically, many couples begin with good intentions and end with bad results because they fail to walk continuously with God. The marriage of Solomon and Abbi had the worst possible last day despite the most incredible first day.

Solomon's entire extended family had suffered greatly because of polygamy. When God created marriage,[18] it was solely for one man and one woman by His divine design. Polygamy started with Cain's godless son Lamech,[19] and every time it was practiced in Solomon's family, it caused great pain and problems for generations. Those who experienced pain because of it included Abraham, who brought forth the nations of Jewish and Arab peoples. This divided family still has conflict 4,000 years later as nations of their descendants continue warring in an ongoing family feud caused by two sons with different mothers but the same father. Polygamy

---

18 Genesis 1–2

19 Genesis 4:19

was temporarily stopped by God in the days of the Flood, when only Noah and his wife, along with his three sons and their wives, survived. Polygamy was literally judged and ended in the Flood and not possible for those who were saved through the judgment. In the New Testament, leaders are told to be "the husband of one wife" to set the example of a healthy marriage for church members.[20] Jesus also has one bride, the Church, and He does not have an intimate relationship with other religions, as that would be spiritual polygamy.

Solomon himself was born to parents who had committed adultery. His father, King David, spied Bathsheba bathing, and he seduced and impregnated her. Bathsheba's husband, Uriah the Hittite, was a good man who served in David's army. While this man was risking his life to protect the king and kingdom, David was taking the forbidden fruit of his wife. To cover his sin, David had Uriah brought home from the battlefront, hoping he would sleep with Bathsheba and then falsely believe that the child she bore was his. However, Uriah refused to enjoy his wife because his fellow soldiers did not have the same pleasure with their wives, and he returned to battle. So David had him murdered, further breaking seven of the Ten Commandments by worshipping sex as god and committing sexual idolatry, murder, adultery, stealing, lying, and coveting. The child conceived in adultery died, but David and Bathsheba had another son—Solomon.

If anyone understood the pain of marital infidelity, it should have been Solomon and Abishag. In 1 Kings 1, King David is on his death bed, and a young woman is brought to care for him. Verses 3–4 say, "So they sought for a beautiful young woman throughout all the territory of Israel, and found Abishag the Shunammite, and brought her to

20 1 Timothy 3:2, 12

the king. The young woman was incredibly beautiful, and she was of service to the king and attended to him, but the king knew her not" (ESV). As we established earlier in this book, Song of Songs is written from King Solomon to a beautiful Shunammite woman. Solomon had a brother named Adonijah, whose mother was Haggith, one of David's other wives. There was a brutal conflict between these two sons of David to succeed their father as king. Solomon took the throne, and after Adonijah asked to marry Abishag the Shunammite, the new king became incensed and had his brother killed (1 Kings 2). If Solomon did in fact marry Abishag, then he saw the pains of polygamy and understood why it was vital to remain faithful to his first wife, who should have been his only wife. Before we judge him, we need to ask ourselves the ways in which we, like he, are carrying on the generational curses, foolish decisions, and sinful patterns that our family has had for generations.

Thus far in our study of the Song of Songs we have seen the man and woman fall in love, plan their wedding, enter into a covenant marriage in the sight of God with family and friends present, and consummate their covenant in what is a near picture-perfect, fairytale love story. Some years later, we read of this horror story in 1 Kings 11:1–11:

> Now King Solomon loved many foreign women, along with the daughter of Pharaoh: Moabite, Ammonite, Edomite, Sidonian, and Hittite women, from the nations concerning which the LORD had said to the people of Israel, "You shall not enter into marriage with them, neither shall they with you, for surely they will turn away your heart after their gods." Solomon clung to these in love. He had 700 wives, who were princesses, and 300

concubines. And his wives turned away his heart. For when Solomon was old his wives turned away his heart after other gods, and his heart was not wholly true to the LORD his God, as was the heart of David his father. For Solomon went after Ashtoreth the goddess of the Sidonians, and after Milcom the abomination of the Ammonites. So Solomon did what was evil in the sight of the LORD and did not wholly follow the LORD, as David his father had done. Then Solomon built a high place for Chemosh the abomination of Moab, and for Molech the abomination of the Ammonites, on the mountain east of Jerusalem. And so he did for all his foreign wives, who made offerings and sacrificed to their gods.

And the LORD was angry with Solomon, because his heart had turned away from the LORD, the God of Israel, who had appeared to him twice and had commanded him concerning this thing, that he should not go after other gods. But he did not keep what the LORD commanded. Therefore the LORD said to Solomon, "Since this has been your practice and you have not kept my covenant and my statutes that I have commanded you, I will surely tear the kingdom from you" (ESV).

To be sure, some of Solomon's marriages were political to unite kingdoms, but he should have remained faithful to God's Kingdom rather than constantly seeking to expand his own. Now, before we use the Bible as binoculars to see Solomon's sexual sin, we first need to use it as a mirror to see our own. Many people have seen far more naked women than he did due to the prevalence of pornography in our day. Many people have a harem on their phone much bigger than the one in his palace, and Jesus said that adultery of the heart counts just as much as adultery of the hands.[21] The additional tragedy is that many men today don't marry or care for the women they sleep with and the children they sire. When kids are involved, it destroys future generations due to fatherlessness and father wounds. Men need to get married, stay married, and love their wives and kids!

If you are a bit stunned, then you are not alone. Solomon was the wisest man after Jesus Christ. He was richer than Bill Gates, smarter than Albert Einstein, more powerful than the President of the United States, and more influential than the Pope. He even had a bigger harem than Hugh Hefner.

So what happened?

Surely, Solomon was not stuck in some loveless marriage with a woman he did not enjoy. Quite the contrary, his wife was amazing, but he wrecked his relationship with both his bride and his God. He should have remembered his own words from Proverbs 5:18–19:

> Let your fountain be blessed,
>   and rejoice in the wife of your youth,
> a lovely deer, a graceful doe.
> Let her breasts fill you at all times with delight;
>   intoxicated always in her love (ESV).

By the end of Solomon's life, the amazing wife he sings to and rejoices in throughout the Song of Songs is gone forever, replaced by a parade of satanic sex and demonic deception. He turned his back on God and let sex become his god.

---

21 Matthew 5:28

If You Stop Walking with God, You Might Start Walking with Demons

If the love story of the Song of Songs were a Hollywood fable, it would end, "And they lived happily ever after." God's Word, however, is rawer and more honest than what we would expect. Solomon simply stopped walking with God and eventually starting walking with demons, feeding his lust and pride. Whether it's forbidden fruit or forbidden females, Satan is always lurking and tempting.

Many of Solomon's other wives practiced false, demonic religions, and eventually the same man who built the Temple for the Lord also built places for the worship of demons. Solomon worshipped demonic false gods with his many wives, had forbidden sex that likely extended beyond his 700 wives and 300 concubines, and encouraged others, including God's people, to do the same. Through the tithe from God's people, he paid for the equivalent of a one-stop-shop cult, strip club, and abortion clinic because all those practices were part of the idolatry of the false gods. The list in Scripture of the exact demons he worshipped is terrifying.

Ashtoreth (also known as Venus) is the Canaanite goddess of sex often worshipped with her male counterpart Baal, with sex being part of their cultic worship. Just like our day with landmarks, icons, and signs to let people know where churches and businesses are, this sex cult put up large poles in the ground atop high places. These were intended as phallic symbols to let everyone know where to go to find the most sinister sex along with demonic worship. Ashtoreth was one of many ancient demons considered the "holy ones" or sacred prostitutes, and idols representing her were often nude, pornographic, and scattered throughout the near east.

89

Milcom (also known as Molech) was the demonic chief god of the ancient Ammonites. The Bible mocks him with the Hebrew equivalent of his name meaning "shame." The Ammonites counterfeit worship involved both sex and the sacrifice of children, including firstborn sons, which is really a mockery of Jesus Christ, the firstborn Son of God who died to save sinners.[22] They even sacrificed their own children by burning them in fire as if they were placing them on the flames of hell,[23] despite this practice being strictly forbidden by God.[24] Even Mesha, the king of Moab, sacrificed his firstborn son as a burnt offering to Molech.[25] Molech was such a powerful demonic force that those who worshipped him seduced many of God's people into sexual sin, "whoring after Molech."[26] After Solomon's father conquered the Ammonites and their demons in battle by the power of *Yahweh*, they "took the crown of Milcom ... the weight of it was a talent of gold [roughly 70 pounds], and in it was a precious stone; and it was placed on David's head."[27] Solomon's worship of this demon god is a complete betrayal of both his God and father along with the kingdom he inherited from both. A Bible dictionary says that on the place they sacrificed their children, "Solomon built Milcom a worship site (1 Kgs 11:5, 33), which Josiah later tore down along with other sites built by Solomon in worship to demons (2 Kgs 23:13)."[xxi]

Chemosh was the ancient demon god and national deity of the Moabites, which is the people from whom Ruth was saved. Scholars believe that the female counterpart of Chemosh was the demon goddess Ishtar (also called Astar, or the Mother

---

22 Leviticus 18:21; 20:2–5; 2 Kings 23:10; Jeremiah 32:35

23 2 Chronicles 33:6; 2 Kings 16:3; 21:6

24 Leviticus 18:21; Jeremiah 32:35

25 2 Kings 3:26–27

26 Leviticus 20:5

27 2 Samuel 12:30; 1 Chronicles 20:2 (NRSV)

Goddess). This demon god and demon goddess were said to have an intense and perverted sexual relationship and were to be worshipped in sanctuaries that were counterfeits of the Temple Solomon built for the worship of *Yahweh*. Because everything God creates, Satan counterfeits, they also had pagan priests whose duties included overseeing the sexual orgies at the temple, and not only sacrificing animals but also children to the demon gods of sex.[28]

These demon gods may be uncomfortable to discuss, but they were all real, and Solomon allowed them into the kingdom and encouraged their worship. We are battling the same demons today, and they want to do to the marriage of Christians what they did to the marriage of Solomon and Abbi. We must never forget that Satan did not even show up and attack our first parents, Adam and Eve, until after their wedding. In

> **WE MUST NEVER FORGET THAT SATAN DID NOT EVEN SHOW UP AND ATTACK OUR FIRST PARENTS, ADAM AND EVE, UNTIL AFTER THEIR WEDDING.**

another book we wrote on spiritual warfare called *Win Your War*, we emphasized that according to the Bible, after the wedding comes the war, and spiritual warfare starts in your marriage. This truth is tragically and grossly on display in the sinful sex of Solomon. He serves as a sobering and frightening example of what any one of us is capable of if we take our sin and our God too lightly. If you have already started down the same path of destruction, the longer you wait, the darker, grosser, and deadlier each step becomes. Today is the day for

---

28 2 Kings 3:27

you to turn around, which is repentance, and run to God for forgiveness and restoration.

We do not know if Solomon ever repented of his obvious sexual and spiritual sin. It is debated, but he may have written Song of Songs when he was young and in love for the first time, collected Proverbs throughout his life, and sat down to write Ecclesiastes as a bit of a repentant look back on the sins of his life. In Ecclesiastes 2:1, he speaks of wasting many years on pleasure saying, "I said in my heart, 'Come now, I will test you with pleasure; enjoy yourself'" (ESV). Looking back as a guilty and lonely old man, he says in Ecclesiastes 9:9, "Enjoy life with the wife whom you love, all the days of your vain life that he has given you under the sun, because that is your portion in life and in your toil at which you toil under the sun" (ESV). This may have been Solomon's attempt at repenting and owning his years of treasonous behavior against his God and his wife, but we simply do not know whether he was repenting or living in regret and remorse (and there is a difference).

God granted Solomon one wish for anything he desired, and Solomon chose wisdom, which pleased God.[29] Next to Jesus, Solomon was the wisest man who ever lived; he was a master of innumerable subjects, and he wrote 3,000 proverbs, 1,005 songs, and three books of the Bible. His power was unparalleled as he reigned as king over Israel for roughly 40 years during a season of peace and prosperity, in which leaders from all over the earth visited his kingdom to inquire of him. He also oversaw the construction of God's Temple and his own palace that took seven and thirteen years, respectively. His complicated family life included his 700 wives and 300 concubines. He could have literally eaten three meals a day, each with a different wife or concubine, for roughly an entire year.

---

29 1 Kings 3:1–5; 2 Chronicles 1

Gifted with unparalleled wisdom as history's salutatorian second only to Jesus Christ, Solomon devoted his life to answering that great question of every brooding teenage punk band member and their midlife crisis parent: what is the meaning of life? Solomon took the adage "Don't knock it 'til you try it" to the absurd by throwing himself with reckless abandon into everything life had to offer, serving as his own subject in the lab of life. If Bill Gates, Stephen Hawking, and Hugh Hefner somehow morphed into one man who was also simultaneously pope and president, then that person might be named Solomon.

Solomon's story may be one a of a prodigal son. Born into the affluence of his father, David, Solomon departed the ways of his God to indulge his own pointless passions. The fact that he wrote Ecclesiastes shows he recognized the folly of his wayward ways, returned to the Lord, and wrote an honest autobiography of the empty and shallow life he had discovered apart from God. Solomon sought the best that life had to offer, and then he realized that nothing rivals life simply lived in obedience to God.

Bored and burned out at the end of his life, Solomon summed up his great life experiment with one word that appears 37 or 38 times in the 12 chapters of Ecclesiastes, depending upon which English translation you read. The book opens and closes with the Hebrew word *hebel*, which is nearly impossible to nail down in its essential meaning. Different Bible scholars translate the word in a variety of ways from "meaningless" (NLT, NIV), to "vanity" (ESV, KJV, NASB, NKJV, RSV, NRSV), to "emptiness" (NEB). Elsewhere in the Scriptures, *hebel* refers to a vapor that is wispy, fleeting, elusive, and quickly passing. This word reveals that life must be pursued with great urgency, because the days between birth and death pass like the mist of a breath on a cold morning.[30] If we layer the various translations, it makes sense that our fleeting life is complex, so a complex word best describes it.

While Ecclesiastes' emphasis on life as meaningless is dark, there's also a clue not to be missed. This is the perspective of life "under the sun." This phrase appears roughly 29 times in Ecclesiastes, depending upon which translation you read. It means life viewed solely without a connection to God or revelation from Him. It's literally a godless life lived by our limited insights gleaned solely by our experience without any word from God on the matter. To use a word from conservative grandmas who read their Bible, this is a "worldly" view of life. It is life as the world sees it, not as God sees it.

In the end, there are only two ways to live: we invite heaven down into our life and marriage, or we pull hell up into our life and marriage. As a young man, Solomon started by inviting heaven down, and heaven did come down when he opened the Temple to lead people in the worship of God.[31] The Song of Songs is the record of his heaven-down first marriage. The rest of the Scriptures we have studied show his hell-up life as an older man. You and your spouse need to decide if your marriage will be heaven-down or hell-up and if your last day of marriage will be the best day or the worst day of your marriage. That's the sobering lesson we learn comparing the first and last day of Solomon and Abbi's marriage.

Three timeless marriage truths will help you prepare for all your days until your final day. First, if you walk away from God, then you are capable of the worst kinds of evil. If a man, whose father wrote and was featured in significant sections of

---

30 Psalm 144:4; Job 7:7, 16

31 2 Chronicles 7:1–16

> **YOU AND YOUR SPOUSE NEED TO DECIDE IF YOUR MARRIAGE WILL BE HEAVEN-DOWN OR HELL-UP AND IF YOUR LAST DAY OF MARRIAGE WILL BE THE BEST DAY OR THE WORST DAY OF YOUR MARRIAGE.**

the Bible, grew up to write three books of the Bible, rule the nation of Israel, marry an amazing wife, rebuild and open the Temple to worship God ... if that man ended up worshipping demons with sex and child murder, while collecting a total of 1,000 other women, then we need to soberly assess our own vulnerability to wrongdoing. Unless we walk with God every day, the evil and destruction we are capable of is terrifying.

Second, blessing and cursing continue for generations. The decisions that others made before we were born greatly impact our lives, whether positively or negatively. In the future, people who are not yet born will also be dealing with the implications of the decisions we are making right now. Therefore, in addition to the life we live, we must constantly consider the legacy we will leave. It is haunting to consider the opportunity God gave Solomon and Abbi, and the pain Solomon caused his wife, as well their children, through his selfish and sinful decisions.

Third, the couple that worships and prays together lays and stays together. Sadly, it is commonly misreported in the media that there is no statistical difference between Christian and non-Christian marriages. That is simply untrue. Bradford Wilcox is among the leading sociological researchers on men, marriage, and family in America. To summarize his years of research in the simplest format, couples who worship different gods have the highest divorce rates, but couples who worship Jesus Christ as the only God have the lowest divorce rates and the highest marital satisfaction rates. If couples walk the

Christian walk and don't just talk the Christian talk, then they have more sex, more joy, more hope, more friendship, less adultery, less abuse, less grief, and less divorce. If you both stay in the Bible, in the Spirit, in the church, in prayer, in worship, in repentance, and in forgiveness, then you will greatly increase your odds of marital success. Not following this way of life is precisely why Solomon's marriage ended in misery. God gave us two hands for one reason: to hold hands with God and our spouse and to walk through life together. When we let go of God's hand, we eventually let go of our spouse's hand as well, as Solomon did.

> **IF COUPLES WALK THE CHRISTIAN WALK AND DON'T JUST TALK THE CHRISTIAN TALK, THEN THEY HAVE MORE SEX, MORE JOY, MORE HOPE, MORE FRIENDSHIP, LESS ADULTERY, LESS ABUSE, LESS GRIEF, AND LESS DIVORCE.**

The Last Day of Your Marriage Can Be Your Best Day

Having studied Solomon's negative example, we wanted to conclude this chapter with a positive example. The last day of your marriage can be your best day and set an example for future generations to have godly marriages that leave godly legacies.

Years ago, someone we knew well began sharing with us the final season of their father's life. Their mother and father had been faithfully married to one another as Christians for more than 50 years. Their dad was diagnosed with cancer, and despite every medical effort, his prognosis became terminal with no hope of recovery barring a miracle. He was determined to run through the finish line of his life, love his wife, and set an example for his grown children and grandchildren.

Despite being in pain and losing strength and health bit by bit as his last day on earth approached, this man was determined to bless everyone in his family, starting with his wife. To bless her, he had a new roof put on their house, hired contractors to do any and all possible home maintenance, and bought her all-new appliances. He knew she would be living without him, so he did all he could to reduce any possible burdens upon her. He wrote out all his passwords and financial information so she could easily pick up on the bill paying and financial organizing he had taken care of throughout their marriage. He made sure his life insurance was paid up so she would be financially secure. He prayed with her every day. He also recorded a series of videos for her in which he relived all the best memories she had given him and all the reasons he was blessed by his wife. He recorded similar videos for all his children and grandchildren, along with Scriptures and prayers to place a blessing over them.

This man made sure that the last day of his life was an incredible day for his wife and set an example of marriage for his children and grandchildren. Some months following his death, on their wedding anniversary, his wife was surprised to hear a knock on her door. A floral delivery person brought her a gigantic bouquet of flowers with a hand-written note from her deceased husband. He paid to have flowers delivered to her every year on their anniversary and penned hand-written notes to be delivered with the flowers. This man not only loved his wife every day of his life but also every day of *her* life. Even after he died and went home to be with the Lord, this man loved and blessed his wife. His example is an encouragement and the model we want for our marriage and for yours. To help you prepare to have a great last day of your marriage, please have a prayerful conversation starting with the following questions that we hope will open your hearts open and help you start planning.

FACE-TO-FACE QUESTIONS
for Couple Discussion

1. If you are engaged, then what are your hopes for your first night in bed together? If you are married, then what are your fondest memories from your wedding day?

2. Husband, look your wife in the eye and in very specific details tell her what you find most attractive about her and why you love her. Wife, simply receive his words.

3. Wife, look at your husband and in very specific details tell him what you appreciate and respect about him. Husband, simply receive her words.

4. Wife, how can your husband make you feel more secure and safe in your sexual relationship?

5. Husband, how can your wife more overtly initiate sex and invite you to pursue her in the ways she likes?

Chapter 5

MY BELOVED
5:2 – 6:1

She

5:2 I slept but my heart was awake.
Listen! My beloved is knocking:
"Open to me, my sister, my darling,
my dove, my flawless one.
My head is drenched with dew,
my hair with the dampness of the night."

3 I have taken off my robe—
must I put it on again?
I have washed my feet—
must I soil them again?

4 My beloved thrust his hand through the
latch-opening;
my heart began to pound for him.

5 I arose to open for my beloved,
and my hands dripped with myrrh,
my fingers with flowing myrrh,
on the handles of the bolt.

6 I opened for my beloved,
but my beloved had left; he was gone.
My heart sank at his departure.
I looked for him but did not find him.
I called him but he did not answer.

7 The watchmen found me
as they made their rounds in the city.
They beat me, they bruised me;
they took away my cloak,
those watchmen of the walls!

8 Daughters of Jerusalem, I charge you—
if you find my beloved,
what will you tell him?
Tell him I am faint with love.

Friends

9 How is your beloved better than others,
most beautiful of women?
How is your beloved better than others,
that you so charge us?

She

10 My beloved is radiant and ruddy,
outstanding among ten thousand.

11 His head is purest gold;
his hair is wavy
and black as a raven.

12 His eyes are like doves
by the water streams,
washed in milk,
mounted like jewels.

13 His cheeks are like beds of spice
yielding perfume.

His lips are like lilies
Dripping with myrrh.
14 His arms are rods of gold
set with topaz.
His body is like polished ivory
decorated with lapis lazuli.
15 His legs are pillars of marble
set on bases of pure gold.
His appearance is like Lebanon,
choice as its cedars.
16 His mouth is sweetness itself;
he is altogether lovely.
This is my beloved, this is my friend,
daughters of Jerusalem.

Friends

6:1 Where has your beloved gone,
most beautiful of women?
Which way did your beloved turn,
that we may look for him with you?

There is a well-known phrase that summarizes the reality that marriage is hard work. At some point, the high wears off, the tough times come, and we say, "The honeymoon is over." On the honeymoon, we are free from all our daily duties so we can focus on our beloved—serving one another, making memories, and having fun. Then we come home to do our laundry, pay our bills, make our meals, and take out our trash.

Two sinners in a fallen, cursed world opposed by demonic forces are bound to have some rough patches. We say this not to discourage you but to encourage you. Just because you have some bad days does not necessarily mean you have a troubled marriage.

> ## "JUST BECAUSE YOU HAVE SOME BAD DAYS DOES NOT NECESSARILY MEAN YOU HAVE A TROUBLED MARRIAGE."

You will have fights—every married couple does. We had our first fight on our first date. We were just 17 years old and still in high school, headed out for the first time. We had gotten to know each other a little bit through conversations on the phone and through seeing each other in our high school hallways. We had exited my car to head for a meal at a burger joint downtown when Grace asked me to unlock the vehicle because she had forgotten her wallet. I asked her why she needed her wallet, and she said to pay for her meal. I was not going to let that happen, so I told her I would not unlock the car because I would buy her burger. We were playfully disagreeing, but then Grace reached for my car keys, which fell to the ground and down a sewer grate, out of sight. She nervously laughed and said we might need to get my other set of keys. I nervously informed her that we had just lost my *only* set of keys. We figured out a plan to retrieve the keys and went into local businesses to get a flashlight, magnet, and long string. Eventually, our sudden scavenger hunt worked out, and we had our supplies. The plan was to use the flashlight to see the key and lower the magnet down on the string to get the key. We executed the plan to perfection with one exception: the key was aluminum so the magnet could not pick it up! So I called my dad, who was a construction worker, and he drove downtown with tools so we could remove the grate, climb down into the sewer like a Teenage Mutant Ninja Turtle, and retrieve the key. If you think this is odd, some years later, on our 20th anniversary when we were in California, the same thing happened ... to the very day of our first date!

If we are honest, which we should be since our marriage ministry is called Real Marriage and not Perfect Marriage, we tend to fight before we have marriage ministry to do. Whether it's writing a book together, speaking at a conference together, or recording our Real Marriage podcast together, the truth is that spiritual attacks come, and we sometimes limp into those ministry moments as we are having our own struggles. We do love one another, but we sometimes respond in ways that aren't helpful in building the marriage.

Thankfully, the most passionate, incredible, and hopeful book of the Bible about marriage includes a genuine marital spat. The Bible is the most honest book ever written, and real marriages have real fights. One of the reasons we know that God and not people wrote the Bible is the fact that people would not be as honest as the Bible is about how badly we human beings mess things up, especially in our marriages.

Selfish or Servant?

Before we jump into the couple's fight in the Song of Songs as a case study for understanding our own marital fights, we should be reminded that the underlying issue for them (and for all of us) is selfishness. Rather than serving one another, they resort to selfishness, and we can all relate to this tough truth.

The key to making marriage work is for both the husband and wife to commit continually to serving one another in love. In Mark 9, Jesus taught some guys arguing over who was the greatest that the person who serves is the greatest. In Mark

10:45, Jesus then taught that He did not come to be selfishly served but instead to serve selflessly by giving His entire life for the benefit of others rather than for Himself. The key to a Christian marriage is to be served by Christ and then serve our spouses like Christ serves us.

> **THE KEY TO A CHRISTIAN MARRIAGE IS TO BE SERVED BY CHRIST AND THEN SERVE OUR SPOUSES LIKE CHRIST SERVES US.**

Everything in this life works against helping us to be servants. When we are little, our parents, grandparents, teachers, and coaches serve us. The teen years are often characterized by great selfishness. Things only get worse in our 20s as we have freedom, money, and no one to whom we are accountable or responsible. We eat what we want, go where we want, watch what we want, and do what we want without considering anyone else. Any tasks we don't like doing, we attempt to find ways to pay other people to serve us and do the work for us, which explains the entire segment of our workforce called the service industry.

Eventually, two people who have spent their entire lives being served get married, and they expect their spouses to serve them. This situation leads to a lot of marital conflicts, and things get even more challenging with children, who are completely helpless and need to be served. The problem is both the husband and wife often look to be served, but they do not want to serve. The sooner this problem is recognized, the sooner their healing begins.

Everyone lives on a continuum from selfishness to servanthood. Three kinds of marriages fall somewhere along that line.

1. **Selfish + Selfish = a brutal marriage**
   Two selfish people end up keeping score for everything from chores to sex, and like a competitive business negotiation, they want to get more than they give. This is a lose-lose arrangement because as the two spouses both seek to win by taking rather than giving, they both lose.

2. **Selfish + Servant = an abusive marriage**
   If one person is always giving and the other person is always taking, then the relationship becomes exhausting and lonely for the person who feels like they are a bank that gets robbed every day. This win-lose arrangement eventually becomes a lose-lose when the giver gets fed up with the taker and walks away from the relationship because it is abusive.

3. **Servant + Servant = a beautiful marriage**
   If both the husband and the wife try their best to consider one another, serve one another, care for one another, and lift burdens for one another, then the result is a beautiful marriage. By striving to live as one, so that when your spouse wins you also win, a marriage can be blessed, healthy, safe, and life-giving.

Sociologists tell us that most divorces happen by the eighth year, which lends some truth to the concept of the seven-year itch.[xxii] It then takes most couples between 9 and 14 years to go from "me" to "we," as they stop being selfish and start serving one another. The quicker this lesson is learned by both the husband and wife, the better the odds for a marriage that is endearing and enduring.

Selfishness is the opposite of love. A person cannot simultaneously be both selfish and loving. However, a person can be simultaneously loving and serving. Taking the famous section on love—probably the most read Scripture at weddings—from 1 Corinthians 13:4–7 (NLT) and personalizing it will help us see ways in which we are selfish and unloving.

1. "Love is patient." (When am I impatient with my spouse?)

2. "Love is kind." (When am I unkind to my spouse?)

3. "Love is not jealous." (In what ways am I jealous of my spouse rather than happy for their blessings?)

4. "Love is not boastful." (Does my spouse hear me mainly talking about myself?)

5. "Love is not proud." (Does my spouse experience me as a proud, unteachable person?)

6. "Love is not rude." (How am I rude to my spouse?)

7. "Love does not demand its own way." (How does my spouse find me inconsiderate?)

8. "Love is not irritable." (When am I grumpy and moody?)

9. "Love keeps no record of being wronged." (What bitterness am I holding onto and using as a weapon against my spouse?)

10. "Love does not rejoice about injustice but rejoices whenever the truth wins out." (What unjust and untruthful things do I do and say to or about my spouse?)

11. "Love never gives up." (When have I given up on my spouse and our marriage?)

12. "Love never loses faith and is always hopeful." (What parts of my spouse and our marriage have I lost hope of ever improving?)

13. "Love endures through every circumstance." (In what circumstances do I use an excuse to give up and stop trying to love my spouse?)

The Bible is a book many people like to study. Because the Holy Spirit wrote it and reveals from it, the Bible is the one book that studies you. Now that we have allowed the Bible to study our hearts and marriages, we will study it to learn from the life and marriage of the Peasant Princess.

A Royal Marriage Rumble

In this section of the Song of Songs, we see what happens when both the husband and wife are selfish. Solomon stays at work way too late, misses dinner and bedtime, and comes home expecting to have his wife waiting for him and ready for sexual intimacy, despite it being near the time of sunrise as his hair is wet with morning dew. Meanwhile, Abbi has fallen asleep and locked the bedroom door to punish him for coming home late. He tries to pick the lock and get in, and she makes feeble excuses for not getting up to unlock the door, such as not wanting to get her feet dirty (which wouldn't happen in the king's castle anyway). Even if it were true, no husband would consider that a deal breaker for lovemaking, or being naked, which is just a way of teasing him. His trying to get the key into the lock may be a double entendre for also wanting to have sex with his wife.[32]

---

32 Isaiah 57:8, 10; Jeremiah 5:31; 50:15

109

There are numerous ways we sexually reject our spouses. First, we do as Abbi did and find a way to lock the door and keep them away. Second, we sabotage bedtime by picking a fight, starting a big project, failing to groom ourselves so we are unattractive or unclean, or staying up alone to avoid being together. Third, we do as little as possible so that sex is boring and predictable to discourage it from happening. Fourth, we do not flirt or initiate sex, which forces our spouse to take the risk of initiating as we do not welcome or encourage their advances.

Every honest married couple understands this scene. One person gets sick of waiting for the other, goes to bed alone, and does anything they can to not have sex to punish their spouse for not doing what they wanted. This is simple selfishness as Abbi does not want to serve her husband, Solomon, by getting up to open the door, and he is selfish to want sex right now even though Abbi is asleep. Sound eerily familiar?

These times of rejection grant Satan a genuine opportunity to cause bitterness that leads to sexual sin. Hebrews 12:15–16 warns married couples, "See to it that no one fails to obtain the grace of God; that no "root of bitterness" springs up and causes trouble, and by it many become defiled; that no one is sexually immoral or unholy."

Eventually, Solomon gives up and leaves, and Abbi falls back to sleep. This is common because when most men see a fight starting, they tend to walk away. When we argue to win, nobody wins, but when we talk through an issue to serve and understand each other, the marriage can grow closer. In marriage the two become one, so a fight between a husband and wife is like the left side of your body fighting with the right—there's no real winner unless you seek mutual understanding.

When Abbi awakens, she expects to find Solomon sleeping on the couch but realizes he has left the house, and she has no idea where he has gone. Frantic, she heads out to search for him and asks the royal staff and their friends if they have seen him, which they have not. Her mention of being mistreated while searching for her husband could be one of two scenarios. First, she could have run off in a frantic moment searching for her husband alone and encountered some bad people who gave her trouble. Second, since she was in that state between awake and asleep for part of this scene, it may have been something of a nightmare where her fears manifested in a semi-conscious state.

When we are hurt, bitter, or selfish, we are prone to develop a negative narrative about our spouse. When a negative narrative is established, all data is interpreted in the worst possible light, and a case is built against our spouse. This is the opposite of love that does not keep a record of wrongs, which Paul addresses in 1 Corinthians chapter 13.

> **WHEN WE ARE HURT, BITTER, OR SELFISH, WE ARE PRONE TO DEVELOP A NEGATIVE NARRATIVE ABOUT OUR SPOUSE.**

When Abbi's friends ask her why she turned her husband away, she comes to the realization that they were both being selfish, and she has a good husband who should not have been locked out of his own bedroom. She reminds herself that her husband is a 1 in 10,000 kind of guy, a real stud with incredible hair, lovely eyes, a great face, and a chiseled body as evidence that he is not allergic to sit ups. At this point in their marriage, they are not perfect spouses, but they are good to each

111

other, and generally speaking, they have a good marriage. Thankfully, Abbi comes to her senses and sees the relationship as more important than the issue. Marriages that place issues above the relationship usually implode. Whatever issue you have, the relationship is more important.

When we struggle with an issue that threatens to implode the marriage, the people we invite to have a view and voice of what is happening and how we should respond are crucial. The worst thing we can do is leak or vent about our spouse to whomever is in front of us, find people who will take our side and arm them with one side of the story so they can join us in battle against our spouse, bring extended family members into the private details of our married life, or post online to welcome anyone on the earth to be part of our family. Abbi's friends serve as a good example of why it is important to have your counsel *before* your crisis and identify the godly people whom you can turn to for wise counsel. Her "friends" appear throughout the book to give godly and safe wise counsel. They remind her that her husband is her "beloved," that she needs to find him and reconcile, and that they want to help her do that very thing. Wise counsel are people filled with the Spirit who are not for or against you or your spouse but are always for the will of the Lord. They are always trying to help you walk in God's will for your life and marriage. Her friends are that kind of wise counsel, helping to save a marriage in crisis as a selfish king and his frustrated wife are in danger of making awful decisions that could destroy their relationship.

My Lover ... My Friend

In this scene, Abbi gives one of our favorite definitions of marriage in the entire Bible, referring to Solomon as her lover and friend, or what was the original Hebrew version of a married friend with benefits. Various English translations of Song of Songs 5:16 include "my beloved ... my friend," "my love ... my friend," "my darling ... my friend," and "my lover ... my friend."

Friendship in marriage is like gravity. It pulls the couple together, even in tough times of trial when failures or frustrations try to pull us apart. According to the wife, it was their friendship that pulled them back together after their fight and their night apart.

The Christian understanding of God is unique compared to all others in the world. The Trinity is the revelation that the Father, Son, and Spirit are friends who love, serve, and do everything together unselfishly. God made us in His image and likeness, and then He said it was not good to be alone, which is the only thing said to *not* be good before sin entered the world. Although our first father, Adam, had God above him and lower creation beneath him, Adam did not have a friend or peer alongside him. So God made the woman from the side of the man and brought them together to be lovers and friends. Satan then showed up to attack them, and he does the same thing today in your marriage. The key is to keep investing in your friendship with God and your spouse. Our friendship with God gives us the pattern and resources for a healthy relationship, thanks to the Holy Spirit.

Friendship between a husband and wife is absolutely crucial to a healthy and successful marriage. Too many religious people settle for functional marriages that lack fun.

John Gottman, one of the most respected sociologists studying marriage today, has come to a crucial conclusion:

> The determining factor in whether wives feel satisfied with the sex, romance, and passion in their marriage is, by 70 percent, the quality of the couple's friendship. For men, the determining factor is, by 70 percent, the quality of the couple's friendship. So men and women come from the same planet after all.[xxiii]

Gottman continues:

> Happy marriages are based on a deep friendship. By this I mean a mutual respect for and enjoyment of each other's company. These couples tend to know each other intimately—they are well versed in each other's likes, dislikes, personality quirks, hopes, and dreams. They have an abiding regard for each other and express this fondness not just in the big ways but in little ways, day in and day out ... Friendship fuels the flames of romance because it offers the best protection against feeling adversarial toward your spouse.[xxiv]

The Bible talks a lot about love in the context of marriage. When Jesus said to love your neighbor,[33] we should assume that love should begin with your nearest neighbor—your spouse. When we love someone, we build a friendship with them. Love is the root, and friendship is the fruit of a healthy marriage.

Over the years, we've had the honor of meeting with people to hear stories of those who have lost their spouse to

---

33 Matthew 10:19; 22:39; Mark 13:31; Luke 10:27 (ESV)

> **THE KEY IS TO KEEP INVESTING IN YOUR FRIENDSHIP WITH GOD AND YOUR SPOUSE.**

the grave, and we've been blessed to pray for them and seek to comfort them. The marriages that lasted the longest and seemed the healthiest had one curious thing in common: a simple and sweet friendship. In hearing people talk about why they missed their departed spouse, what was mentioned most was the loneliness of losing their companion and best friend. Holding hands, sharing laughs, going for walks, eating meals, snuggling on the couch, laying hands on and praying over one another, and worshiping together are things we've heard over and over. The older you get, the more you learn that life is a lot less about *what* happens and much more about with *whom* it happens. You cannot choose the family you were born into, but you do choose your spouse, which makes marital friendship a sacred honor.

Economists and sociologists like to distinguish between our financial capital and our social capital.[xxv] Just as we have a limited amount of wealth to put into our monetary investments, so too we have a limited amount of life to invest in relationships. A friendship is a costly investment. There is an important distinction between being friendly and being friends. As a general rule, it is good and godly to be friendly toward all people and only friends with a few. Our first two relational priorities must be a healthy relationship with our God and then with our spouse. This was the pattern in the beginning when Adam and Eve had a worship relationship with God and were brought together to begin their marriage relationship with one another. All other relationships follow these two, and our priorities need to follow this biblical pattern. Friends are people we uniquely share things with, and our spouse should be our nearest and dearest friend.

Friends share loyalties. We honor our friends whether they are present or absent; we do not betray them. They can depend on our commitment to their well-being and our devotion to one another. When loyalties are tested, true friends pass those tests. A good friend is a burden-lifter in a world filled with burden-givers.

Friends share stories. We talk about the best moments of our friends' lives, not their worst. When we speak to or about them, we seek to build their reputation up rather than beat it down like enemies do. A good friend walks in the door when everyone else is walking out.

Friends share memories. We do life with our friends, from the mundane (like going to the grocery store) to the magnificent (like going on an epic vacation). We take photos and videos so we can look back at the times we shared, both laughs and tears together, as friends are woven into the very fabric of our lives. A good friend makes a bad day half as bad and a good day twice as good.

Friends share resources. We give gifts to our friends, we are generous with our friends, and if they need something and we have it, we gladly give or share it. Our blessing comes from seeing our friends blessed; when we share, we are blessed, and so is the friendship. A good friend is there for you when you have nothing to give, and they want to give you everything they have.

Friends share intimacies. We let our friends know parts of us that no one else knows. We trust them to hold in a relational bank vault of sacred confidence our biggest regrets, deepest fears, and strongest hopes. True friends do not gossip about us, and they know it is treasonous to take private matters public, especially online. Good friends pour courage into you when life has drained it out of you.

Most marriages start as friendships between intimates and sadly deteriorate into partnerships between roommates. No marriage has constant red-hot passion, but a healthy marriage has those moments and is sustained and carried by the warmth of friendship.

3 Kinds of Marriages

For many years we have distinguished between *three kinds of marriage relationships* and how the best ones are face-to-face friendships:

1. **Shoulder-to-shoulder**: These married couples are good at projects, chores, tasks, and working together to get things done. Every marriage has a lot of shoulder-to-shoulder work that needs to be done in the daily tasks of life. Some seasons, like an emergency or crisis, the raising of children, or the building of a house or business, more intensely push a couple to live shoulder-to-shoulder. The focus is on a common task, which shifts the priority from loving one another to laboring with one another. We are incredibly good at shoulder-to-shoulder marriage. Since our dating years we have worked well on the job together, and we have done home remodels, church plants, and nonprofit ministry startups. We have raised five kids, written books, given lectures, and much more. If we are not intentional with pursuing face-to-face time, we can get stuck in a shoulder-to-shoulder connection, which eventually turns us back-to-back.

2. **Back-to-back:** These married couples have spent too much time and energy shoulder-to-shoulder instead of face-to-face, and they are lonely and weary. This comes out in frustration, being "sick" of each other, or even having contempt toward one another. Back-to-back couples avoid one another as much as possible. When life presses them together, a lot of anxiety and even conflict ensues. Many marriages seemingly function, even if they are not fun, in the shoulder-to-shoulder arrangement so long as the children are still living at home. Once the children leave, though, the married couple no longer has the shared task of constant parenting, and it can throw their marriage into a crisis. Sensing this, some couples do all they can to keep their kids from growing up and moving out by over-parenting, or they pressure their adult children to give them grandchildren. If you stop investing in the friendship and communicate only through fighting, this back-to-back position ultimately hardens your hearts toward each other. Bitterness sets in, and romance leaves.

3. **Face-to-face:** These married couples remain devoted to building their friendship in every season of life no matter what. They get in each other's worlds, do life together, share hobbies, and are partners in all of life. Being face-to-face is the Bible's language for friendship. The old theologians from the early days of the Protestant Reformation talked about living life *Coram Deo,* which means 'in the face of God.' Moses's friendship with God is reported in Exodus 33:11, which says, "The LORD used to speak to Moses face to face, as a man speaks to his friend" (ESV). In the

Kingdom of God, our eternal friendship with Jesus is described as seeing Him "face to face" (1 Corinthians 13:12). Just as your lungs need air, so too your marital friendship needs face-to-face time where you lovingly look at, speak with, and listen to each other. God's divine design for marriage explains why couples in love can spend hours gazing into one another's eyes when they are together and use technology, including photos and videos, to do the same when they are apart. Even our most popular love songs echo this theme—"I Only Have Eyes for You," "Your Smiling Face," "The First Time Ever I Saw Your Face," "I Grew Accustomed to Her Face," "Have You Seen Her Face, and "The Face I Love."

A pivotal moment came many years into our marriage. I (Mark) would get home from an overwhelming day, and Grace would try to engage and support me by saying, "Tell me about your day." Honestly, I knew her intentions were good, but there were many times that the very last thing I wanted to do was relive the details of a bad day, since it felt like returning to a crime scene or revisiting a haunted house. One night, the kids were asleep, and as we sat on the couch face-to-face, she asked a slightly different question: "How can I be a good friend right now?" Like most men, I have a lot of relationships but not a lot of friendships. Most of the relationships men have are shoulder-to-shoulder, as the relationships we have are those we play sports with, serve in the military with, or work alongside. Whereas most women don't feel awkward being face-to-face with girlfriends, it's weird for most dudes. This is why guys go to sporting events, ride in a golf cart, or sit at a bar to watch a game—to avoid being face-to-face with our buddies. For most men, a face-to-face friendship with a wife is a new gift and something of a new skill they need to learn.

Today, our phones and other screens are constantly demanding our attention, causing us to ignore our spouses right in front of us. This includes pornography, private communication with people with whom we are tempted to sin, and social media where we begin to peer in on and fantasize about other people. This problem is so widespread and problematic in marriage that psychologists have created a diagnosis called "phubbing."[xxvi] One guy in Vegas even married his phone in 2016.[xxvii] At some point, we all likely feel jealous of our spouse's phone as they are so devoted to it. We always know where our phone is and what energy levels it has. We carefully tend to its safety and well-being, and we will drop everything we are doing if it notifies us that it requests our attention (usually with a beep or a ring). Sadly, most smartphones are better cared for than spouses.

The Gottman Institute describes the best way to shift from being face-to-face with your smartphone to face-to-face with your spouse:

> Try taking 30 minutes together, face-to-face, as a trial run without phones. Notice how different your interactions and conversations feel when you can see each other's facial expressions and make eye contact, which will give you an indication of how much more connected the two of you may be when spending time device-free. Express how you feel after those 30 minutes and try to build that routine into your daily life with your partner. Outside of 30 minutes of daily device-free time, silencing your phone during dinner, or even leaving it in another room, is a good habit to get into

so you can focus on the meal and on your partner and/ or family. You can make an agreement with your partner on when and where smartphones will be allowed or not, and there are apps that you can use to monitor how much time you're spending on the phone, especially if you'd like to cut back on device usage overall.[xxviii]

In this scene of Song of Songs, the couple works through their fight, focuses on their friendship, and has a loving, healing conversation face to face. This talk results in intimate lovemaking because once their souls and hearts are connected, their bodies naturally follow. Often, problems in the bedroom are fixed by a friendship outside the bedroom. When sex is about performance and not connection, there's a lot of pressure that can make things too serious and self-conscious. This is what Abbi means by calling Solomon her friend and lover. Friends have fun together and are not thinking that sex needs to be like an Olympic performance with a panel of judges; rather, it is just another way that married friends have fun.

> **WHEN SEX IS ABOUT PERFORMANCE AND NOT CONNECTION, THERE'S A LOT OF PRESSURE THAT CAN MAKE THINGS TOO SERIOUS AND SELF-CONSCIOUS.**

For example, there was a couple we knew some years ago, and they were both timid and shy. They had some things they wanted to try sexually but never really mentioned or initiated those things. They sat down and talked about how much they meant to one another as friends, and how they wanted not to be so shy and timid about sex. They went shopping together for new furniture, and she flirtatiously said they should have sex on the coffee table when they got it home. A few days later he came home from work and was happily surprised to see her laying on the coffee table. The story ends with them breaking the new coffee table! As they lay together on the floor atop the broken coffee table, they reported having one of the greatest laughing fits of their marriage, because that's what friends do!

Life is constantly pushing your marriage shoulder-to-shoulder, and the enemy is constantly pushing your marriage back-to-back. You will both need to remind yourselves continually to work toward face-to-face. To help that happen, we've prepared the following discussion questions for your face-to-face time together with your phones and other technology turned *off.*

FACE-TO-FACE QUESTIONS
for Couple Discussion

1. Why did you pick each other as friends and spouses?

2. What are some of the specific examples in the past when your spouse was a great friend to you?

3. How can you be a good friend to each other this week in specific ways?

4. What are some specific things that are not helping build your friendship?

Chapter 6

MY DOVE
6:2 — 6:10

She

6:2 My beloved has gone down to his garden,
to the beds of spices,
to browse in the gardens
and to gather lilies.

3 I am my beloved's and my beloved is mine;
he browses among the lilies.

He

4 You are as beautiful as Tirzah, my darling,
as lovely as Jerusalem,
as majestic as troops with banners.

5 Turn your eyes from me;
they overwhelm me.
Your hair is like a flock of goats
descending from Gilead.

6 Your teeth are like a flock of sheep
coming up from the washing.

Each has its twin,
not one of them is missing.

7 Your temples behind your veil
are like the halves of a pomegranate.

8 Sixty queens there may be,
and eighty concubines,
and virgins beyond number;

9 but my dove, my perfect one, is unique,
the only daughter of her mother,
the favorite of the one who bore her.
The young women saw her and called her blessed;
the queens and concubines praised her.

Friends

10 Who is this that appears like the dawn,
fair as the moon, bright as the sun,
majestic as the stars in procession?

———————

When we were on our honeymoon, we checked into a cute little bed and breakfast that was just a short bike ride down a dirt path from the Oregon coast. The woman who owned the inn felt like God told her to say something to us. We did not know her, nor did we know she was a Christian until that moment, but what she said to us was from the Lord. We were standing side-by-side, and she asked us to hold hands. Then she said we needed to never consider each other an enemy, but Satan was going to attack our marriage and lie to us, hoping to convince us that our spouse was our enemy. He would tempt us not to stand together for our marriage against our real enemy, the devil. It seemed like an odd thing to say, since at the time we were newlyweds, but it is absolutely true.

Division literally means two visions, and Satan did not even attempt division on earth until our first parents were married, as the first division was between a husband and wife, which ruined the world.

Fast forward, after being in ministry for over a decade with five children, we were having an argument one night in the bathroom, out of earshot from the kids who were in bed. It felt like we were stuck in a cul-de-sac of misunderstanding and frustration. We didn't know how to stop! As I (Grace) was praying in my head for help and wisdom, the Holy Spirit told me, "Tell him you aren't his enemy!" I was confused as to what that meant and argued in my head for a moment. The Spirit urged me again, "Tell him you aren't his enemy!" So I said it to Mark, and he replied, "Yes, YOU are!!" I was stunned. I had no idea, nor did he, that he actually had been deceived by the real enemy into thinking I was against him. All I knew was how hard (though still imperfectly) I had worked to love and respect Mark as my husband, so this could only be explained as the deceptive work of Satan. I quickly replied, "Well, that's the problem." When Satan can convince one or both spouses that *they* are the enemy, then he can sit back and watch the fights rage on. When together we expose *him* as the enemy and pray for the Lord to help us walk in unity, then we have the opportunity to experience healing, peace, and joy in our marriage. I had no desire to be the divider of our marriage, but with unhealed hurts and the enemy's deception, that was how it played out. We talked it

WHEN SATAN CAN CONVINCE ONE OR BOTH SPOUSES THAT THEY ARE THE ENEMY, THEN HE CAN SIT BACK AND WATCH THE FIGHTS RAGE ON.

through and dug up any roots of bitterness so we could walk in forgiveness and mutual understanding. I was so thankful the Holy Spirit exposed the unholy spirit that was trying to steal, kill, and destroy our marriage.

Taking Every Thought About Your Spouse Captive

At this point in the Song of Songs story, Solomon and Abbi have reunited after their fight and returned home, and they are trying to figure out how to repent of their sin and forgive the sin of their spouse. Things have calmed down, and they are no longer back-to-back but instead sitting down face-to-face to reconcile their relationship.

Emerging brain science is finding that we actually have distinct parts of our brains.[xxix] When we are feeling emotional, unsafe, anxious, upset, or hurt, we process what we are thinking and feeling in a part of the brain that is more reactive than reflective and more emotional than reasonable. We all know what it is like to be in an argument from this part of our brain. We can feel some things that, when later processed, were untrue or exaggerated. We can say some things that are unreasonable, and we later regret and feel bad about them. When the husband and wife are dealing with an issue in this part of their brains, it usually ends with a nuclear-sized mushroom cloud over their house. They turn back-to-back until the systems in their body recalibrate so they can process their issue(s) in another part of the brain. This part of the brain makes us act like children for a time and produces reactions the Bible negatively refers to as "the flesh." In our flesh the enemy takes weakness and inputs lies, division, and opposing desires to the unity God has for our marriages.

The other part of the brain is more the adult part. For a couple to work through a contentious issue, it is commonly said there must be at least one adult in the room, which is now being proven by brain science. This separate part of the brain processes information more accurately and reasonably, has empathy to see the other person's side, and is more reflective, contemplative, and logical. This part of the brain is also more reasonable and spiritual. When we have a conflict, as Solomon and Abbi did, we tend to start in the front brain, which contributes to a harsh startup of the conversation.

When the Bible talks about renewing our minds[34] and taking every thought captive in obedience to Christ,[35] it is actually working from another part of our brain than the one we operated in when acting childish. Instead of believing everything we think or feel is true, we bring it before the Lord. The language of taking a thought captive in obedience to Christ comes from ancient military language. When a person was captured in war, they would be brought to the highest-ranking officer for interrogation to get the truth out of them. Since Satan is the father of lies, we need to take every thought we have, especially about our God and our spouse, and bring it to Christ to have it interrogated to see if it is true or false. Lies are powerful deceptions that create an alternate reality and bring demonic oppression into a marriage. The way to test these negative thoughts is by Scripture, prayer, and wise counsel, all guided by the Holy Spirit. The moral of the story is we cannot believe everything we think.

A helpful tool in taking every thought captive and making it obedient to Christ comes from Marcus Warner's book *Understanding the Wounded Heart*. In it he explains there are

---

34 Romans 12:2

35 2 Corinthians 12:5

> ## THE MORAL OF THE STORY IS WE CANNOT
> ## BELIEVE EVERYTHING WE THINK.

four C's: *confess, cancel, command, and commit.*[36] Start by confessing any lies you are believing about God, yourself, or your spouse. In the name of Jesus, cancel these lies and any foothold they have been given, and command the demonic spirits responsible to leave and take all their works and effects with them. Finally, commit yourself to truth and what the Word of God says, and invite the Holy Spirit to empower you for life in the truth. If you follow this process regularly as you detect lies and spiritual warfare, then you can keep short accounts and bring peace, unity, and healing into your marriage relationship.

Connect Before You Correct

At this point in the Song of Songs, the couple is back at a more reasonable place, responding out of the better halves of their brain, and ready to sit down and build up each other and the marriage. To *encourage* someone literally means "to pour courage into them."

When a couple is fighting, they can err on one of two sides:

1. They can *lack the courage to be honest* about how they and/or their spouse caused pain and harm. If you are afraid of other people, absolutely hate conflict, or would rather avoid someone than have a difficult conversation, then this is your tendency. When we first married, this was Grace.

---

36 Adapted from Pastor Karl Payne's book Spiritual Warfare.

2. They can *overreact and speak harshly* in a way that beats the spouse down rather than building them up. If you wait until you are so upset that you blow like a volcano, get louder and more intense when you are frustrated, or vent at the wrong time rather than waiting for the right time, then this is your tendency. When we first married, this was Mark.

The key to having a happier, holier, and healthier conversation about something painful or problematic is to begin by stating the positive things you appreciate about your spouse to encourage them. Then you can both have the courage and patience to discuss and resolve the things that are negative.

What Solomon and Abbi model in this scene is the principle of "connect before you correct." If your relationship is stuck in either shoulder-to-shoulder or back-to-back, then any correction will seem like negative criticism, punishment, or controlling and domineering manipulation. This principle explains why firing off a text or email, leaving a salty voicemail, yelling at someone through the phone, or posting your critique online never results in someone opening their heart and ears for correction. There can be no godly, healthy, or loving correction unless there is first connection. The latest brain science calls this principle "attachment theory." This big idea aligns with the Bible in that until you believe someone loves, likes, and is for you, you cannot be attached to them. This truth played out in our previous story of me thinking Grace was my enemy and wasn't for me—we didn't feel "attached."

If you remember the couple's fight in the Song of Songs, then it started with him being out late at work and coming home to find her locking him out of the bedroom. Abbi teased Solomon a bit, which increased his sexual frustration, so he left, and she could not find him. If you've been married for more than 15 minutes, you've likely experienced something similar. In the next chapter, we see them do a lot more than just kiss and make up.

Since Abbi was likely the primary person responsible for this fight, it makes sense that she speaks first. She reiterates her love for Solomon and devotion to him, and she declares that they belong together: "I am my beloved's and my beloved is mine" (6:3). This mutual belonging is how a couple fulfills God's plan for unified oneness and stands against Satan's plan for division and destruction.

Seeing that the conversation is going to be a safe one and that Abbi's goal is for them to belong to and take loving care of each other, Solomon stops fighting and starts flirting. Reminding her of his affection and attraction, he likens her beauty to two magnificent ancient cities. *Tirzah* in Hebrew means 'to be pleasing,' and it may have been a place where they enjoyed romantic getaways. Jerusalem is called "the perfection of beauty" (Psalm 50:2). It's clear that Solomon is reassuring Abbi that despite a bad night, they are not going to have a troubled relationship. Since a woman's deep need is security, he affirms that his love for her is unchanged despite a tough time.

Solomon then repeats the comments he made to Abbi during their dating relationship, honeymoon, and early years of marriage. He still finds her "beautiful," "lovely," "majestic," "perfect," "unique," and "blessed." Gazing at her face, he flirtatiously mentions the loveliness of her eyes, hair, teeth,

> **SINCE A WOMAN'S DEEP NEED IS SECURITY, HE AFFIRMS THAT HIS LOVE FOR HER IS UNCHANGED DESPITE A TOUGH TIME.**

and face. His words are filled with the familiar nicknames like "my dove" and "my perfect one." As they gaze into one another's eyes, they are looking into each other's hearts, and they return to God's heart for their marriage.

Jesus said that Moses permitted divorce because of the hardness of hearts.[37] Everyone, no matter how godly they are, has a hard heart toward their spouse at some point. Being married to someone with an ongoing hard heart for a prolonged period is incredibly difficult because it seems that no matter what you say or do, it only makes their heart harder and their response meaner. The legendary hard heart in the Bible belonged to Pharoah. Roughly half of the time, the book of Exodus says God hardened Pharaoh's heart, and the other half of the time it says he hardened his own heart. Pharaoh is a case study in hard-heartedness—he continually hardened his heart against God and Moses. Every time God sent Moses to speak the truth to him kindly, warn him, and invite him to repent and have a change of heart, Pharaoh got more angry, defiant, and unyielding. The result was God's loving and patient grace further hardened Pharoah's hard heart. The Bible is clear that becoming a Christian is getting a new heart. God can and does changes hearts, so we need to bring our hearts to Him for spiritual heart surgery when they are hardened.

When someone has a hard heart, the relationship is back-to-back, adversarial, and unsafe. When someone is hard-hearted toward their spouse, it means they are also hard-hearted toward their God. This is true because we've only got one spiritual heart, and from it all of life flows.[38] When Abbi repents as they sit face-to-face in Song of Songs, Solomon sees that her heart is tender and not hard. When she sees the love

37 Matthew 19:8

38 Proverbs 4:23

in his eyes and forgiveness in his voice, she sees that his heart is tender and not hard. Thankfully, our God has chosen to forgive our sin so we can have relationship with Him. He sent His Son so we could see the loving face of our Savior and know the heart of God that is always devoted to us. Our relationship with God is our most important relationship, and how God treats us is how He wants us to treat our spouses.

Throughout this Bible study together, our homework has been to ask you to meet together face-to-face. We see the couple in Song of Songs often meeting face-to-face to discuss their relationship in and out of the bedroom. A lot of what we communicate to our spouse is nonverbal. There is an entire industry based on reading body language, which is used to train everyone from police officers to soldiers, government agents to therapists. There are entire books and classes that train specialists to read facial expressions. In this scene from Song of Songs, their face-to-face time together brings forgiveness, healing, and restoration. We want the same for you, which is why lots of healthy face-to-face time is a blessing to your marriage.

Forgiven People Should be Forgiving People

In Song of Songs, both the husband and wife are now dealing with their sin. Abbi punished Solomon by locking him out of his own bedroom, and he ran off without communicating to her, causing her anxiety. They both sinned against one another. The reason God put a marital fight in the Bible is to show us that it's going to happen in our marriage too. Every couple sins against one another. From this example, we can learn a lot about how to deal with our sin against our spouse.

Before we think about the sins our spouse has committed

> **THE REASON GOD PUT A MARITAL FIGHT IN THE BIBLE IS TO SHOW US THAT IT'S GOING TO HAPPEN IN OUR MARRIAGE TOO.**

against us, it is helpful to consider our sins against God first. The Bible is clear from beginning to end that everyone who has ever walked the earth, other than Jesus Christ, is a sinner both by nature and choice. Proverbs 20:9 asks the humbling rhetorical question, "Who can say, 'I have kept my heart pure; I am clean and without sin'?" Romans 3:22–23 says, "There is no distinction: for all have sinned and fall short of the glory of God" (ESV). Biblical images for sin include rebellion, folly, self-abuse, madness, treason, death, hatred, spiritual adultery, missing the mark, wandering from the path, idolatry, insanity, irrationality, pride, selfishness, blindness, deafness, a hard heart, a stiff neck, delusion, unreasonableness, and self-worship.

Sin includes commission (we do what is forbidden) and omission (we don't do what is commanded). It includes thoughts and motives that only God truly witnesses as well as words and deeds that our spouse also witnesses. Sins are deeper than crimes because God's laws go further than governmental laws, which explains why you cannot call the police when your spouse lies to you. Sin is total depravity, and it infects and affects all our being—body, mind, will, soul, emotions—so there is not any part of us that is pure and without the stain of sin. This is much like food coloring being added to a glass of water so that it colors all the water in the glass.

As sinners, we not only sin, but we also respond sinfully to our sin in a variety of ways. We minimize our sin, trying to get others to see it as less awful than God says it is. We make ourselves the exception to the rule by explaining our extenuating circumstances that we hope excuse us from responsibility. We rationalize our sin by creating self-justifying arguments to defend ourselves. We shift the blame to someone else, wrongly seeking to paint them as the villain and ourselves as the victim. We create diversions where we change the subject or shoot the messenger to move the target from us and on to someone or something else. We partially confess a minor bit of the full truth in hopes that people we have offended forgive us, move on, and do not uncover the whole truth. We double down even when we are wrong in an effort to wear our spouse down and out so that we do not have to own our sin. We paint ourselves as victims of everything from our culture to our personality type, family of origin, or genetics and blame those things for our sin. We practice what Paul calls "worldly sorrow,"[39] where we say we are sorry so that people will move on from our wrongdoing, but we have no real remorse or desire to change.

If we're honest, we are all familiar with these sinful responses to sin in our own lives. Not only is your spouse a sinner, but so are you. Sin is present in every person, and when two sinners get married, they must know what to do with sin if their marriage is to survive. If you can imagine a marriage where the trash is never taken out of the house, then you can imagine the spiritual and emotional equivalent of what happens when a couple does not know how to take out their sin.

The heart of Christianity is that we can have a relationship with God by repenting of our sin, and God forgives our sin through Jesus Christ. Sadly, our culture is so devoted to preaching tolerance of sin that preaching repentance of sin is wrongly seen as unloving, cruel, and mean-spirited. The truth is, the most loving thing a sinner can be invited to do is repent of sin so

---

39 2 Corinthians 7:10

that they can be forgiven and receive a new nature, new identity, new desire for holiness, and new power by the Holy Spirit. God loves us so much that He will take us as we are, but He loves us too much to allow us to remain as we are. Instead, He transforms us to become like Jesus Christ by His love.

> **GOD LOVES US SO MUCH THAT HE WILL TAKE US AS WE ARE, BUT HE LOVES US TOO MUCH TO ALLOW US TO REMAIN AS WE ARE.**

The most famous prayer ever prayed is the Lord's Prayer by Jesus Christ. In Luke 11:4 Jesus said, "Forgive us our sins, for we ourselves forgive everyone who is indebted to us" (ESV). Here, Jesus compares our sin against God to debt. In other religions, the sinner must seek to do the impossible and repay their sin by good works or reincarnating to suffer and pay off the debt. Only Christianity teaches the concept of full forgiveness paid by someone else. When the Bible repeatedly declares that Jesus Christ is the ransom or debt payment for our sin, it means He pays it in full, and we do not repay God at all. This is what is meant by *grace*: that salvation was earned by Jesus and not by us. It is a free gift from Him to us. Jesus lived the perfect life we have not lived, died the substitutionary death we should have died, and rose to defeat the enemy of death we could not conquer. The answer to our sin is Jesus Christ our Savior.

Jesus actually prayed for our forgiveness while dying on the cross in our place for our sins. In Luke 23:34, Jesus said, "Father, forgive them, for they know not what they do" (ESV). This is known as one of the final seven statements of Jesus from the cross. This mention of forgiveness so angered the soldiers overseeing His martyrdom that they took a sponge, put it on a stick, sopped it in wine vinegar, and shoved it in His mouth.[40] In the ancient world, the field kit for a Roman soldier included a sponge that would be used as toilet paper when put on the end of a branch and sopped in wine vinegar as a disinfectant.[xxx] The remaining things Jesus said on the cross were likely spoken with the taste of a soldier's bowel movements on the lips of our Lord. Forgiveness is free for us, but it was costly for Jesus. Jesus then died to answer His own prayer, and we were forgiven.

Looking back on the death and resurrection of our Lord and Savior, Jesus Christ, Paul gives a lot of detailed commentary in his letter to the Colossians.

> And you, who were dead in your trespasses and the uncircumcision of your flesh, God made alive together with him, having forgiven us all our trespasses, by canceling the record of debt that stood against us with its legal demands. This he set aside, nailing it to the cross. He disarmed the rulers and authorities and put them to open shame, by triumphing over them in him (Colossians 2:13–15 ESV).

In the unseen realm, there was a comprehensive list of all our sins that Satan held against us. When Jesus died for your list of sins, he ended Satan's rule over you as a master and began God's adoption of you as a Father.

Just as Jesus paid a price for our sin and suffered loss so we could be forgiven and have a relationship with God, so too we need to do the same for our spouse (to a lesser degree). Jesus' bride, the Church, caused Him a lot of real pain, and our

---

40 Matthew 27:48; Mark 15:36; John 19:29

spouse will cause us some real pain too. Jesus suffered a lot for our marriage, and we will suffer a little for our marriage. There will be moments that feel like we're getting crucified a little bit and are paying a price for our spouse's sin. And when we forgive them, we are suffering loss so that our relationship with God and our spouse can win.

> ## JESUS SUFFERED A LOT FOR OUR MARRIAGE, AND WE WILL SUFFER A LITTLE FOR OUR MARRIAGE.

How God treats us is how we are to treat our spouse. The big idea is that *forgiven people must be forgiving people.* Forgiveness is not just a gift God gives us, but one He gives us to also share with our spouse. Colossians 3:13 says, "As the Lord has forgiven you, so you also must forgive" (ESV). In the next section, Paul goes on to give directives for Christian husbands and wives, but he first lays the foundation of forgiveness of sin because without it, there can be no relationship.[41] Paul follows this same pattern in Ephesians where he talks at length about forgiveness through the Holy Spirit in chapter 4 and then goes on to talk at length about marriage in chapter 5. The point is simple: until you learn about repentance of sin and forgiveness for sin, you are not ready to be married.

The simple equation for our relationship with God and our spouse is as follows:

Repentance + Forgiveness = Healthy Relationship

41 Colossians 3:18–25

In the remainder of this chapter, we will study this more deeply and apply it more frequently. Again, this is precisely what we see in the Song of Songs, which we are using as a marital case study. They have sinned against one another, need to repent to one another, and must forgive one another if their marriage is going to be healed and restored.

Learning to Row in the Same Boat

If you've ever tried to go boating together with your spouse using oars, then you quickly learn that there's three options, and only one works. First, you can both *not* row, and the result is that you go nowhere and are stuck indefinitely. Second, one of you can row but not the other, and the result is that you go around in circles. Third, you can row together, each pulling on your oar, and make forward progress that builds momentum.

Since a husband and wife are in the same boat, they need to learn how to use the oars of repentance and forgiveness. Repentance is what we do wrong—when we sin, act foolishly or selfishly, and hurt our spouse. Forgiveness is what we do when they wrong us. It does not matter which person pulls on their oar first; for there to be a loving, healthy marriage relationship, both the husband and wife need to learn how to use both oars.

Sin

Repentance and forgiveness of sin require us to first understand sin. Not everything that annoys us in marriage is a sin. Sin is violating what God wants, which is a vastly different thing than our spouse violating what we want.

For starters, there is a substantial difference between sins and mistakes. A sin is a violation of the Word of God, will of God, and ways of God. A mistake is just part of being human. To be sure, mistakes can be frustrating, expensive, and inconvenient, which is why they trigger an emotional response. When a mistake is made, however, we need to remember that how we feel is likely not how God feels. This is what Colossians 3:13 means by saying, "Make allowance for each other's faults" (NLT).

For example, when our five children were little, the boys kept trying to ride their bikes or electric kid-sized Jeep to a local donut shop on the other side of a highway. To corral the free-range boys, we bought an expensive rolling gate to close off the driveway and secure the boys. Forgetting to tell Grace I had pulled the new gate closed, she jumped in her large SUV and backed into it (she didn't have a backup sensor, and the gate was below her line of sight), denting her car and the new fence. She came up to my office to tell me what happened, and unlike a lot of times where I got it wrong, this time I got it right. I said, "Everybody makes mistakes. Sorry for not telling you it was closed." When sins and mistakes are treated the same, a marriage is characterized by an impossibly constant, demanding pressure for perfection, which is stressful. Humans sin, but it's not a sin to be human.

Sins are not minor offenses. Every person has their uniquely quirky series of oddities. The longer you live, the more you learn how annoying you can be. In marriage, the love should be all the time, even though the sin is some of the time, which is why, "love covers a multitude of sins."[42] Some couples err in not dealing with many marital issues, which causes a lot of unspoken and unhealed pain and hurt. Other couples err in dealing with pretty much everything. If either

42 1 Peter 4:8 NLT

141

of you cannot forgive and forget, move on, overlook, and give grace, then every day of your marriage will feel like a performance review with your own live-in Pharisee.

Sometimes we are simply irritable, grumpy, and on edge because of things that have nothing to do with our spouse. When the Bible says that "love" is "not irritable,"[43] it means that just because we are in a bad mood does not mean our spouse has done a terrible thing.

Sometimes our spouse is just having a bad day and says or does something out of character that we need not make into a case against them but just flush and forget. The best version of us usually does not show up when we are in the hospital, have the flu, or have been up all night with a sick kid. On the day we get fired, our parent dies, or we total our car in a wreck, a little bit of grace goes a long way. Proverbs 19:11 says, "Good sense makes one slow to anger, and it is his glory to overlook an offense" (ESV).

Repentance

The **oar** of repentance is:

- **O**wning your sin
- **A**pologizing for your sin to God and your spouse
- **R**eversing your sin so that the future is different than the past

Repentance is a combination of owning your sin, apologizing for your sin, and reversing your sin. Real repentance does not partially confess some of the facts while concealing

---

43 1 Corinthians 13:4–5 NLT

others—it tells the *whole* truth. Real repentance does not make excuses but instead makes changes. Real repentance does not blame anyone or anything for sin. Repentance understands that if Jesus died for something, then it's a big deal, and if we don't deal with it, then it will kill our marriage.

Repentant people are safe people. Repentant people are honest not just about others but also about themselves, and they are humble enough to deal with reality and have compassion and empathy for how their decisions impact and affect their spouses.

When we repent to God for sinning against Him, our God forgives us. When our spouse repents to us for sinning against God and us, we need to join our God in forgiving them. Sadly, religious people like to weaponize repentance by not granting forgiveness. They will demand a list of signs or evidences to prove repentance so they can remain in a position of a controlling and demanding judge, which is a position reserved solely for God. Or they will put their forgiveness at the finish line of some long, detailed, and painful process of proving repentance rather than at the starting line. Actions like these are the opposite of love and grace because you must work *for* them rather than work *from* them to live a new life. God begins by loving us, forgiving us, giving us grace, and entering into a relationship with us that helps us change. God does not put those things at the finish line but rather the starting line of the relationship. Religious people do the opposite and want grace for themselves while they give law to everyone else. Jesus called this the plank-speck game.[44] This is ungodly precisely because it is unlike God. The truth is, we can forgive our spouse even if they don't repent and let God deal with them instead of us.

---

44 Matthew 7:1–5

Forgiveness

The **oar** of forgiveness is:

- **O**vercoming the sin to have a healthy relationship
- **A**ccepting their repentance as genuine
- **R**eleasing your spouse from vengeance through punishment or payment

Forgiveness is not shallow words you say but what you deeply believe as you "forgive ... from your heart" as Jesus taught.[45] Forgiveness is not excusing their sin, denying their sin, pretending it never happened, or blame shifting the wrongdoing to someone or something else.

The opposite of forgiveness is unforgiveness. Unforgiveness has many names—hurt, disappointment, woundedness, grudge, beef, an ax to grind, resentment, bitterness, broken-ness, and carrying an offense. Unforgiveness is the opposite of love. When we keep a record of wrongs, we are acting as an accountant and keeping score of the spiritual debt others have accrued to us. This is why unforgiving people say things like "They owe me," "I will make them pay," or "I will get even."

We have seen *seven types of bitter believers* in our decades of ministry together.

1. The **archeologist** is constantly digging up past sins that are buried with Christ, because they have not forgiven.

2. The **one and done forgiver** acts as if Jesus got it wrong saying we should forgive "seventy times seven"[46] and should have said "one times one".

---

45 Matthew 18:35

46 Matthew 18:21–22

3. The **case-builder** takes any recent sin and adds it to the list of all the prior sins in the history of the marriage, even though Paul tells the Corinthians that it's fine to keep a record of what our spouse has done *right* but not good to keep a record of their *wrongs*.

4. The **negative narrative reporter** has established a bad storyline about who we are, and all new information is forced into the negative narrative so that even good things are presented in a bad light.

5. The **bridge burner** wants to create distance or even end the relationship, and they search for offenses to excuse lighting the match to burn the bridge between us.

6. The **broken believer** has suffered a lot of pain and even trauma, which is unhealed and causes them to respond to sin in ways that are broken and unhealthy.

7. The **identity adopter** no longer sees themselves primarily in light of their relationship to God but instead in light of their pain, like Naomi (meaning "sweet") who changed her name to Mara (meaning "bitter") in Ruth 1:20.

When our spouse sins against us, forgiveness can easily seem that it is between us and them. While that is true, our willingness to forgive our spouse is a matter that is between us and God more than between us and them.

> **OUR WILLINGNESS TO FORGIVE OUR SPOUSE IS A MATTER THAT IS BETWEEN US AND GOD MORE THAN BETWEEN US AND THEM.**

Unforgiveness and bitterness were big problems for some years in our marriage. I (Mark) had an inner vow that I made before I met Grace or was even a Christian. An inner vow with yourself is the counterfeit of a covenant with God and is a typical response to pain. Someone or something hurt us, and we want to ensure we will never experience that pain again. Rather than forgiving the people involved and trusting the Lord to be our shield of protection, we make an inner vow. Generally speaking, an inner vow is a "never again" promise we make to ourselves— "Never again will someone say, do, see, or cause this pain I have endured." When someone violates an inner vow, our response tends to be an overly emotional overreaction because past trauma is triggered, which surfaces unhealed and unhealthy fear and anxiety. We feel like we are fine, over a past hurt, or have moved on until something from the past rushes to the present and we feel it deeply all over again as if we were reliving it.

Grace fully repented of her past sin to me, but I did not truly forgive her from my heart for many years. The issue would seemingly be gone but would then resurface with anger and hurt when we had conflicts and disagreements. In numerous ways and in various arguments, I adopted every one of the seven types of bitter believers. I had taught on the dangers of bitterness for decades and preached on forgiveness of sin, yet I failed at times to give grace to my own wife. The point is that you can know about the oars of repentance and forgiveness and even teach other people how to use them, but then not use them yourself, which leaves your marriage dead in the water.

Bitterness, like weeds, has roots. Roots are unseen, go deep, and remain hidden until they burst forth with ugly visible weeds. Anyone who has ever tried to deal with weeds by plucking the top instead of pulling the roots knows that things only get worse until the roots are pulled up. Your life, marriage, and family are like a garden that will have its fruitfulness choked out unless you keep pulling the weeds from the roots. Forgiveness is the only root that can dig deep enough to get to the root of bitterness. Hebrews 12:14–16 says, "Strive for peace with everyone, and for the holiness without which no one will see the Lord. See to it that no one fails to obtain the grace of God; that no 'root of bitterness' springs up and causes trouble, and by it many become defiled" (ESV).

After another argument over a small issue while on vacation, I (Grace) told Mark that he kept bringing up things for which I had apologized and repented. I kindly asked him to pray about whether he was bitter against me because it seemed like he was keeping record of wrong. He said he would pray about it and needed a time of solitude to think. After being gone several hours, Mark returned with a small, vintage green shovel that had a Mason jar attached to the front. Being the visual man he is, he had gone to a craft fair (this is genuinely loving) and an old café to find an old school paper tablet that the waitresses would write your order and bill on. Mark wrote,

> Grace Driscoll's past debt is paid in full,
> and the past will no longer be dug up!
> Romans 8:1, Philippians 3:13–14

This signified that he had dug up his bitterness and forgiven me for good. I hung it up in our bathroom between our sinks, and it's the first thing we see to start every day. Sometimes a visual reminder can help us not fall back into old patterns.

Bitterness Pulls Hell Up. Forgiveness Invites Heaven Down.

When most people go to the doctor, they are told several things that would be good for them to do. Each of those good things usually comes with some price to pay, such as we cannot eat what we want, or we need to stop sleeping in and instead hit the gym on the way to work. In response, most people ask, "What will happen to me if I don't do these things?" They weigh whether the reward is worth the sacrifice.

When it comes to your marriage, life, and family, you've only got two options: you and your spouse live between heaven and hell. Every day, the decisions you make either pull hell up into your marriage or invite heaven down.

In the fight we studied from Song of Songs, the couple started by pulling hell up into their marriage. Thankfully, they sat down to repent and forgive each other, which invited heaven back down into their marriage.

Jesus' half-brother James urges us to not pull hell up into our lives by choosing things like bitterness that are "false to the truth ... earthly, unspiritual, demonic ... and ... vile" but instead to invite heaven down into our lives with the "wisdom that comes down from above."[47] Paul exhorted, "Set your minds on things that are above, not on things that are on earth."[48] Jesus taught us to pray and then live heaven down, not hell up: "Your kingdom come, your will be done, on earth as it is in heaven."[49] When we see demons rise up in our marriages, we are living "hell up," and when we see the Holy Spirit fall on our marriages, we are living "heaven down."

---

47 James 3:14–16 ESV
48 Colossians 3:2 ESV
49 Matthew 6:10

Perhaps the most common way hell comes up into our marriages is through unforgiveness. When the Bible speaks of unforgiveness, it often speaks of the demonic and living hell up. This makes sense as hell is a culture of unforgiveness—it's where all the unforgiven and unforgiving people go. Conversely, heaven is a culture of forgiveness—it's where the forgiven and forgiving people go. When we are hurting and feeling wronged, Satan wants to make us bitter, but God wants us to forgive to make us better.

> **PERHAPS THE MOST COMMON WAY HELL COMES UP INTO OUR MARRIAGES IS THROUGH UNFORGIVENESS.**

In Matthew 18, Jesus tells a parable about a man who was forgiven for a lot but would not forgive someone else for a little. The result was Satan (typified by the jailer in the story) would torment the man who wanted to be forgiven for his sin but would not forgive others of their sin.

In Ephesians 4:26–32, Paul deals with forgiveness. He admits that when we are sinned against, we will be emotional and even "angry," but that's not an excuse to respond to another person's sin with our own sin. Rather than letting our anger simmer for days until it erupts like lava spewing out of a volcano, we should deal with today's problems *today*. Sin in a marriage usually starts with a hot war where our blood is boiling, and the conversation is heated. This is what happened in Song of Songs when Solomon came home to a locked door and a punishing wife. As things escalate, the hot war usually shifts to a cold war, in which we ignore one another, give the silent treatment, put walls up, and have a very cold marriage.

This also happened in the Song of Songs when Solomon leaves their home, and Abbi has no idea where he has gone.

Eventually, Solomon and Abbi sit down face-to-face to have a conversation about their sins against one another, and thankfully it goes well and not poorly. We've all had conversations in which our words were more like punches than blessings. When we are sinned against and frustrated, Paul says we must intentionally "let no corrupting talk come out of your mouths, but only such as is good for building up, as fits the occasion, that it may give grace to those who hear" (Ephesians 4:29 ESV).

At some point, we all spill something we are drinking. Something bumps our cup, and what is inside spills outside. Whatever comes out of the cup is obviously what was already in the cup. Whatever bumps the cup does not change what is in the cup; it only reveals what was in the cup. In me was bitterness, and whenever Grace bumped me, bitterness came out. She did not make me bitter, and no matter how hard she tried to not bump me, eventually she did, which is what we all do to our spouse regularly. I needed to invite God to change what was in me so that grace poured out of me whenever Grace bumped me. This is where the Holy Spirit alone can change what is in us so that grace comes out of us. Like a friend who wants to help and is standing by, when we do not stop to pray, meet with God, and talk to Him about our anger before we talk to our spouse about our anger, we "grieve the Holy Spirit of God" who wants us to "be kind to one another, tenderhearted, forgiving one another, as God in Christ forgave you" (Ephesians 4:32). When we seek forgiveness, we are inviting heaven and the Holy Spirit down into our marriage. When we seek bitterness, we are pulling hell and demonic spirits up into our marriage. On occasion, people will unknowingly admit this, saying in effect,

"Being married to them is hell," which is what happens no matter who our spouse is if we choose bitterness over forgiveness.

Marriage becomes a demonic, lose-lose spiritual war when both the husband and wife choose bitterness. Like any war, the two sides start recruiting people to join their army and gear up for the brutal battle. Our friends, family, coworkers, social media followers, and even our own children or grandchildren are fed our bitterness and opened to the demonic, and we begin bringing curses on other families and generations of our own family. Once the cycle of bitterness is underway, things go south toward hell, as Ephesians 4:31 says, "Get rid of your bitterness, hot tempers, anger, loud quarreling, cursing, and hatred" (GW).

Over the years, we have seen bitter people who have not previously known about each other meet, form an unholy alliance, encourage each other's bitterness, and participate in each other's evil. This often happens, for example, in church and online. Have you ever wondered how this is possible? Although the bitter people do not know one another, their demons do, and the demons introduce the bitter people to one another to form an unholy alliance. Make no mistake, the first front of spiritual warfare is your marriage.

The good news is that no matter how long you have been bitter, you can always invite heaven down by choosing to forgive. When you do forgive, you are engaging in spiritual warfare and disarming the demonic in your marriage. In Acts 7, there is a picture of an early church leader named Stephen who is being martyred by a bitter religious leader named Saul, whom we now know as Paul. While dying, Steven prays for Paul to be forgiven, just like Jesus did while dying on the cross. Stephen then saw heaven open, and Jesus Christ, who normally sits upon His throne, stood up to give a standing ovation to cheer for Stephen. If you want to get Jesus as excited as a sports fan watching a spectacular play, forgive your spouse. Jesus then answered Stephen's prayer, came down from heaven to deal with Saul himself, saved him, forgave him, and gave him a life-long ministry of preaching the forgiveness of sins. The point of this example is that if you forgive your spouse, God will bless you and come down to deal with them Himself. When we hold onto our bitterness, we are rejecting our own blessing and getting in the way of our spouse dealing directly with Jesus. When we forgive them, we stop playing God, get out of the way, and let things get sorted out between them and God. Your forgiveness is the key to God's anointing. You can have your bitterness or God's anointing, but you cannot have both.

> **YOU CAN HAVE YOUR BITTERNESS OR GOD'S ANOINTING, BUT YOU CANNOT HAVE BOTH.**

Do You Want to Be Healed?

There is an interesting question Jesus once asked a man who had been unwell for many years: "Do you want to get well?"[50] At our church, I tell our wonderful people, "The *want* to precedes the *how to*." My point is that telling someone how to get better is of no use unless they want to get better.

Do you want to get better?

Do you want your marriage to get better?

Things either get bitter or they get better.

If you choose forgiveness over bitterness, then it will heal

---

50 John 5:6

your marriage spiritually as we have learned, but it will also heal you physically. One lie the enemy whispers to us when we are offended is that if we choose bitterness, we will hurt those who hurt us. The truth is, we will also hurt ourselves. An ancient Chinese proverb says, "The person who seeks revenge should dig two graves."

When your marriage is in the Spirit, situations work out for a win-win. When your marriage is in the flesh, situations result in win-lose. When your marriage is in the demonic, situations end up in lose-lose. When you choose forgiveness, you both win, and when you choose bitterness, you both lose.

Repenting and forgiving are love in action. Healing starts with repenting and forgiving. At Stanford University, Frederic Luskin ran the Forgiveness Project, teaching and researching forgiveness for many years. He published his findings in the book *Forgive for Good: A Proven Prescription for Health and Happiness.* The book does not have Christian themes like Jesus dying for our sin or having eternal forgiveness in relationship with God. However, the simple concept of working to apply some sort of forgiveness to the pains of life has been clinically proven to reduce anger, hurt, depression, and stress. Physically, things like ulcers, stomach problems, tension headaches, and heart problems are reduced by forgiving. Mentally, forgiveness allows us to stop acting like air traffic controllers with an ever-growing number of unresolved conflicts and hurts flying in our head and instead land those planes to clear our minds and bring a sense of closure. Emotionally, forgiveness allows us to remove our hurt from the center of our dining room, box it up, and put it in the attic of our life where we rarely notice and no longer orient our lives around it. Relationally, forgiveness allows us to stop responding to our pain with hurt, where we isolate, withdraw, or hate, and where we view most everyone with a jaded suspicion, as all our relationships are poisoned by one bitter relationship. Practically, forgiveness allows us to stop making unenforceable rules that the other person will not abide by, thereby triggering our anger and disappointment over and over.

The stress of unforgiveness causes numerous problems as the weak spot in our body is exposed in everything and anything from headaches, stomach problems, ulcers, canker sores, blurred vision, chronic pain, heart trouble, nervous twitches, weight change, elevated blood pressure, and disrupted sleep (we either cannot fall asleep, stay asleep, or stop sleeping). So we try to self-medicate with food, alcohol, sex, porn, caffeine, gambling, shopping, or the diversion that technology affords while we spend mindless hours gazing at some screen for no good reason. In more extreme cases, paranoia, panic attacks, heart attacks, and even suicidal thoughts occur.

The problem with unforgiveness is that it causes the pain in the past to live with us in the present and haunt us in the future. Our bodies are not built for constant stress. God kindly made our bodies to sense danger and respond to preserve our lives. However, it is our minds and not our bodies that have any sense of time, so if our minds are dwelling on a dangerous, damaging, or difficult person or event from 10 years ago, our bodies respond as it were occurring 10 seconds ago. When we don't forgive someone in our minds, we trick our bodies into responding to the past traumas in the present over and over and over. Our brains release various hormones such as adrenaline, and like a car that is turned over and brought to life with all the systems running in harmony on a wintry morning, we are "on," feeling alert, awake, and aware.

This is a short-term survival response that makes perfect sense when you hear a bear nearby in the woods, but it is an overkill response to remembering an offense from your spouse from years prior. Spiritually, forgiveness allows our souls to stop looking back at our worst days and look ahead in faith that good days are before us. The apostle Paul writes in Philippians 3:13, "I focus on this one thing: Forgetting the past and looking forward to what lies ahead" (NLT). When our focus is on someone who hurt us, we are not focused on the God who can heal us and heal our marriages.

When someone has acted like an enemy, even if it is our spouse, we know we have truly forgiven them if we can sincerely bless them. After all, God not only forgives us but also blesses us and wants us to do the same. In fact, blessing is the test of forgiveness according to Jesus.[51] You know you have forgiven someone from the heart when you find ways to bless them. This is precisely what we see in Song of Songs.

Kiss and Make Up and Make Out and...

Returning to Song of Songs, the couple repents after their big fight, forgives, and blesses one another. Their entire conversation consists of encouragement and love, speaking a blessing over one another. This conversation is evidence that they have worked through their pain to a place of healing and warm intimacy in their marriage. If you've ever heard about a couple having a fight and then kissing and making up by making out, then you will understand what happens next in the most erotic, frank, and free section of the entire Bible.

---

51 Luke 6:28

155

FACE-TO-FACE QUESTIONS
for Couple Discussion

Before you meet with your spouse, you need to:

- carve out some time
- turn off your phone
- get alone with God to pray, journal, and verbally process anything you need to repent of to your spouse or for which you need to forgive your spouse.

You need to have the conversation with God before you have the conversation with your spouse. If there is some deep hurt you are processing and needing to forgive, then you may need to write a processing letter that you will not show to anyone, post online, or divulge anything unless it's to someone like a professional counselor helping you with trauma. The point of the letter is to, with full and raw emotion, process your hurt, and then take the time to pray forgiveness for whatever is bothering you from the heart. Have your emotional heart funeral and come to a sense of closure so you can move forward in your healing journey with the Lord. Paul says that love does not keep a record of wrongs (1 Corinthians 13:5). Sometimes this means you make a record of wrongs, forgive the entire list, cancel the entire debt, and instead tear it up or burn it as a way of declaring that it is now gone, done, and forgiven.

After you have met with the Lord, have a private conversation:

- turn your phones off
- look at one another with a lot of love and grace
- have a healthy conversation taking turns owning and repenting of sins against one another
- forgive one another from the heart
- pray for one another without getting angry or having an argument
- dig up your roots of bitterness for the last time

The best thing you can do is be honest and repent of whatever you must and ask your spouse if there's anything you've missed. Since there will likely be some tears, do this in private and keep praying over one another throughout this deliverance date.

Chapter 7

THE DANCE OF MAHANAIM
6:11–7:10

He

 6:11 I went down to the grove of nut trees
  to look at the new growth in the valley,
  to see if the vines had budded
  or the pomegranates were in bloom.
 12 Before I realized it,
  my desire set me among the royal chariots
  of my people.

Friends

 13 Come back, come back, O Shulammite;
  come back, come back, that we may gaze on you!

He

 Why would you gaze on the Shulammite
  as on the dance of Mahanaim?
 7:1 How beautiful your sandaled feet,
  O prince's daughter!
  Your graceful legs are like jewels,
  the work of an artist's hands.

2 Your navel is a rounded goblet
that never lacks blended wine.
Your waist is a mound of wheat
encircled by lilies.

3 Your breasts are like two fawns,
like twin fawns of a gazelle.

4 Your neck is like an ivory tower.
Your eyes are the pools of Heshbon
by the gate of Bath Rabbim.
Your nose is like the tower of Lebanon
looking toward Damascus.

5 Your head crowns you like Mount Carmel.
Your hair is like royal tapestry;
the king is held captive by its tresses.

6 How beautiful you are and how pleasing,
my love, with your delights!

7 Your stature is like that of the palm,
and your breasts like clusters of fruit.

8 I said, "I will climb the palm tree;
I will take hold of its fruit."
May your breasts be like clusters of grapes on the vine,
the fragrance of your breath like apples,

9 and your mouth like the best wine.

She

May the wine go straight to my beloved,
flowing gently over lips and teeth.

10 I belong to my beloved,
and his desire is for me.

———

Some years ago, we moved into a home that was built on an
old apple orchard. Nearly all the trees had been removed for

the building of houses, but two apple trees remained. It just so happened they were in our yard.

Sadly, the apple trees were in bad shape. We were told by an older couple who had lived in the neighborhood for many years that at one point in their past, the trees had been planted, cared for, and pruned, and they produced a bountiful harvest of tasty apples. But those days were long gone. The trees had not been pruned in so many years that their branches were lying on the ground extending in every direction. Sucker branches had also overtaken the tree, redirecting the life and nourishment away from the production of apples. In the spring, there were zero edible apples between the two trees.

Unsure what to do, we called a landscaper who specialized in fruit trees. He explained that the once glorious trees had been neglected for so many years that they needed a very extreme pruning that would shock them. All the unfruitful branches, along with the sucker branches, would need to be cut off completely. This would be a little bit like surgery for the trees, and they would need time to recover. Eventually, however, the trees would start budding again and, in time, growing delicious fruit for our family to enjoy.

A well-tended garden is many things: a private oasis to relax, refresh, and replenish; a place of beauty and inspiration; and a place of nourishment and savory treats. Our first parents got married in a garden, consummated their covenant in that same garden, and were naked and without shame there. Because of sin, they were kicked out of the garden, and ever since, God wants us to make our marriages a little slice of Eden to enjoy life in together.

A lot of marriages are like our apple trees. Early in the marriage, we spend a lot of time tending to our marriage garden, caring for our spouse, pulling up the problem weeds, and pruning out problems. Over time, however, a bit of unforgiveness, laziness, and selfishness settle in. Then kids enter the scene, and we let them displace our spouse as our priority. Or work takes our first and best energy so there is little left to give at home. As this happens over the course of a few seasons, eventually we enjoy the garden of our marriage a bit less and less, and the sex gets worse and worse. Why is this so? Because sex is the fruit of the marriage, and unless you tend to your garden, the fruit will be less and less sweet.

> **SEX IS THE FRUIT OF THE MARRIAGE, AND UNLESS YOU TEND TO YOUR GARDEN, THE FRUIT WILL BE LESS AND LESS SWEET.**

If You Want to Eat the Fruit, Tend the Garden

Throughout the Song of Songs, Solomon and Abbi keep referring to their marriage in terms of a garden and their spicy sex life as fruit of their garden,[52] including apple trees.[53] If you have ever tried to keep a lovely garden, then you understand it takes a lot of work and patience.

You cannot put seeds in the ground, yell at them, and expect them to grow faster. You must wait patiently and water faithfully. Eventually, the plants begin to take root, and signs of life appear. At the same time, weeds are constantly growing, seeking to choke out the beauty of the garden and replace it with ugliness and unfruitfulness. This waiting time requires

---

52 2:3; 4:12–13, 15–16; 5:1; 6:2; 7:8, 13; 8:11–13

53 2:3; 7:8; 8:5

not only tending to your plants but also pulling the weeds.

Eventually, what was planted begins to grow a bit wild. This situation requires strategic and intentional pruning to keep the life and energy flowing toward fruitfulness. Some people, habits, and commitments need to be pruned from the marriage so it can be a priority and have the time and energy to remain a beautiful garden you both enjoy. To state it plainly, marriage is a garden, and both the husband and wife are the gardeners.

At this point in Song of Songs, the couple has been married for some years. They have tended to the garden of their marriage so that it has proven to be a safe place for taking risks, trying new things, and being vulnerable. Every aspect of your marriage should grow over time. Spiritually, you should constantly find ways to care better for one another's souls through being in a Bible-teaching, healthy church community together. Emotionally, you should constantly be improving your friendship and love for one another by being attentive to needs and planning time to have fun together. Physically, you should be constantly getting better at serving one another through helping wherever it is needed. Sexually, you should constantly be improving how you enjoy one another by being creative and pursuing God's gift of sex to us. Like a garden where different plants grow at different rates and some need more attention than others, everything in marriage does not grow at the same pace—some areas need us to focus additional care and energy to cultivate.

In this section of Song of Songs, we arrive at the most frank and free part of the entire Bible. Before we study it, we want to warn you against weaponizing this or any other part of the Bible. In a marriage if someone is domineering and not getting their way, then it is common for them to become religious and quote the verses that help them to get their way.

Religious people abuse the Bible to control people rather than use the Bible to care for people. Throughout the Song of Songs, we will see the fullness of freedom that God gives married couples to explore the fruit of their sexuality. In the Bible, there are descriptive texts that explain what people did and prescriptive texts that give God's commands for people. Prescriptive texts are about our obedience.

In the Song of Songs, many of the bare details are descriptive and not prescriptive texts. Prescriptive texts don't give us God's commands about what we have to do but rather freedom to do what we want to do. The Bible gives us the guardrails of commands and the freedom within those guardrails to live according to conscience. Too many Christians think the Bible is only prescriptive commands *or* descriptive freedoms, but the Bible is both. Like a garden with walls around it to protect and preserve it, God gives us commands to obey. Within the walls of that garden, we can plant what we enjoy and do so freely.

One massive problem in our culture is the separation of sex and marriage into distinct categories. The tragic result is people who want to have great sex but are not as committed to a great marriage. God made marriage as the garden and sex as the delicious fruit that grows in the garden. The goal of a Christian couple should not simply be great sex but rather a great marriage that results in great sex. This is the big idea that weaves the book of Song of Songs together. If you want good fruit, then tend to the garden.

> **THE GOAL OF A CHRISTIAN COUPLE SHOULD NOT SIMPLY BE GREAT SEX BUT RATHER A GREAT MARRIAGE THAT RESULTS IN GREAT SEX.**

What Abbi and Solomon did in their intimate times is explained throughout the Song of Songs, and you are free as a married couple to do the same if you agree to it together. If you do not agree to do those things, then you do not have to do them. The Bible talks a lot about our conscience, which is given by God to help us make decisions. In addition to obeying the Bible, God's people need to heed their consciences. The Bible gives us God's line, and our conscience gives us our line, which is sometimes a few feet back from God's line because we lack self-control and need to be honest about our struggles. The Bible also talks about people who are weak and strong. We are all weak in some areas and strong in others. The Bible repeatedly encourages those who are strong in an area (e.g., drinking alcohol and sexual freedom within the God-given boundaries) to give up a bit of freedom to have a healthy relationship with the person who is weak in that area, because our relationship should be our highest priority. This is especially true of marriage.

For example, when Grace and I married, I (Mark) did not drink any alcohol, and she did once in a while. I had never been drunk, but my conscience forbade me from drinking. Grace could have a glass of wine when we had dinner, and it did not bother me at all—I knew it was not a sin for her, and it was not a struggle for me. She was willing to abstain from alcohol altogether if I had struggled with it, so I gave her freedom to abide by her conscience, and she did the same for me. Almost 10 years into our marriage, my conscience changed, and we now occasionally have a glass of wine together. Your conscience can and does change over time, and the important thing is to make the relationship the priority and not push one another to violate your consciences. This is especially true in our sex life with our spouse, as this is part of tending to our marriage garden.

The Dance of Mahanaim

Abbi was supposed to spend the day with her girlfriends but had a sudden sexual fantasy that she wanted to try with her husband. Rather than continuing her day as expected, she left her friends to go act out her desire with her husband. Her girlfriends don't understand when she leaves abruptly, and she does not explain it for obvious reasons.

There's an important lesson to be learned here. Often, we have a fleeting thought about something sexual we would like to surprise our spouse with, but we do not act on that curiosity. We make excuses for why it's a bad idea, lose our confidence that we can actually be that brave and bold, or wrongly assume that our spouse is too busy or distracted to disrupt their day. She could have had all these inhibitions and more. Her husband, the King of Israel, is busy at work, and she is going to unexpectedly show up and seductively dance a striptease for her husband. She is quite bold and brave, and she is a good example of the need to push through our excuses and pursue our godly passions.

In calling his wife the "Shulammite" (6:13), he is reminding her of where she lived as a young girl, the same place she perhaps cared for Solomon's father, David, as he was dying. It was likely at this place and in this season that they fell in love as Solomon prepared to succeed his father as the leader of Israel, and his heart melted when he saw the selfless young woman caring for his dying father.

Dance of Mahanaim means "to whirl" or spin, Bible resources tell us. One Bible commentator calls it "the name of some dance known to the ancient Israelites."[xxxi] Mahanaim is first mentioned in the Bible as the place where angels had come to visit Jacob,[54] so Solomon is saying that her dancing is angelic and breathtaking. Importantly, as she is taking a significant risk, he is encouraging her with his words so that she knows she is safe with him to explore their full sexual freedom. Abbi is being visually generous allowing Solomon to see a lot, and he is being verbally generous and encouraging her by saying a lot.

One Bible commentator says, "His praise of her beauty moves generally from bottom to top."[xxxii] He compliments her literally from head to toe while she dances seductively in front of her husband. Most Bible commentators find this section too hot to handle, and rather than having their minds transformed by God's Word, one Bible commentator explains the tendency of many who "declines to translate or comment on it at all," and "changes ('corrects') the Hebrew text so it is no longer recognizable."[xxxiii]

In a world filled with a lot of extremely sick teaching about sex, Bible teachers must not blush at what God says. People have real questions, real struggles, and real needs for their real marriages, and if they cannot get real answers from God, then we are leaving them no godly, healthy, or holy options. We need to learn God's Word and not try to edit it, thinking He went too far and needs our help to redraw the lines He put in the wrong place for marital freedom.

> WE NEED TO LEARN GOD'S WORD AND NOT TRY TO EDIT IT, THINKING HE WENT TOO FAR AND NEEDS OUR HELP TO REDRAW THE LINES HE PUT IN THE WRONG PLACE FOR MARITAL FREEDOM.

---

54 Genesis 32:24–32

Here's what this section of Song of Songs actually means:

- Her sandaled feet are "beautiful."

- Her legs are "like jewels, the work of an artist's hands."

- Her "navel" is like "a rounded goblet that never lacks blended wine."
  - This is probably not her bellybutton, for two reasons. First, a large, round, and very red bellybutton is not beautiful but probably infected. Second, he just spoke of her legs and will next speak of her waist, so this reference to "navel" is for a part of her body between her legs and waist, which is not where one finds a bellybutton. The *Faithlife Study Bible* rightly says, "It is probably a sexual euphemism."[xxxiv] Another study Bible says, "Navel may be a euphemism for Shulamite's more intimate sexuality."[xxxv] A Bible commentary says, "If the order of bodily parts, from bottom to top, is followed consistently, the navel is in the wrong position between thighs and belly: it comes above those. The part of the girl's body mentioned here is therefore more likely to be the vagina or vulva than the navel."[xxxvi] Lastly, a Bible scholar says, "It is generally translated as 'vulva.' The description 'never lacks mixed wine' speaks of it as a source of sexual pleasure and moistness."[xxxvii] To state the obvious, the couple frankly and frequently talks about the sex they want to have and then talks while they are doing what they had talked about to encourage one another to full freedom. This is in God's Word because it is something God allows for our pleasure.

- Her "waist" is like "a mound of wheat." When wheat is bundled, it is tied in the middle, which is his way of talking about the shape of her body and how it goes in around her waist.

- Her "breasts" are like "twin fawns," which is a repeat of his prior playful depiction of her as perky and desirable to touch. This is the one section of her body that he mentions more than once, as he will mention it again at the end of this section. One study Bible also says, "Solomon used the metaphor of a palm tree and its fruit to describe his delight in Shulamite's breasts."xxxviii

- Her "eyes" are like the beautiful, deep blue "pools of Heshbon."

- Her "nose" is "like the tower of Lebanon," which seems to mean she has a large nose that he really likes, which works out well for them both.

- Her long "hair" may be up in some sort of braid as it is like a beautifully woven "royal tapestry."

Not surprisingly, the husband can only watch this wonder for so long and can no longer contain himself. In speaking about her body swaying effortlessly like a "palm" tree, he wants to "climb the palm tree," enjoy her "breasts," smell her "breath" and kiss her "mouth" which has the lingering flavor of the "best wine" that they were apparently also enjoying.

With a bit of after play and pillow talk, Abbi says, "May the wine go straight to my beloved, flowing gently over lips and teeth. I belong to my beloved, and his desire is for me" (7:9–10). Likely enjoying a glass of wine as they snuggle together after lovemaking, she speaks last as she is continually straightforward and overt throughout their relationship. This is because she feels secure and safe, and they are solely and mutually devoted to one another.

I (Grace) have found that research has shown security is the number one need for a wife, and this includes emotional, physical, spiritual, financial, and sexual security. Obviously, no husband can fill this need perfectly, but it's a process throughout marriage to build these areas in a healthy way. When a

> **SECURITY IS THE NUMBER ONE NEED FOR A WIFE, AND THIS INCLUDES EMOTIONAL, PHYSICAL, SPIRITUAL, FINANCIAL, AND SEXUAL SECURITY.**

husband sins or falls short in any of these areas, repentance is very healing, rather than excusing or blameshifting. As the wife, we need to work to be a helper who encourages rather than discourages a husband to build security in the marriage. Emotionally, the wife needs to be treated with kindness and consideration, which focuses on words of encouragement and listening well, while valuing her role. Physically, she needs not to worry about harmful actions against her but rather gentle and loving touch and her husband's protection of her. Spiritually, if the husband is leading with God as his head, praying over her, and washing her in the Word, then she will feel secure. Financially, if he is working hard (not lazy) and they are working together to be responsible stewards of what God gives, then it's not about how much money he has but about fiscal wisdom. Sexually, she will flourish when she feels secure in the other areas and not forced or used for sex; she wants to be desired and special. This advice could possibly sound overwhelming to a man, but it's an honor to delight in your wife and a lifetime of joy when you plant security in the roots of your marriage garden. It becomes natural behavior that God honors when we get in the habit of doing things to bless and love our spouses. Wives should be encouragers and not just takers of a husband who wants to create security. This never overrides the biggest place of security for us as husbands and wives in our God who loves us and has a plan for our marriages.

3 Questions to Ask Before You Do "It"

Having just studied the spiciest section of the Scriptures, it might be helpful to recap the fun and freedom Abbi and Solomon have reported so far in the Bible's marriage pyrotechnics manual. So far, we have seen them flirt a lot, enjoy heavy petting, manual stimulation, oral sex, sex, and stripping both indoors and outdoors, at home and in other non-public places during fun getaways. In reading about their freedom, you probably have your own questions that start something like, "Can we do 'it,' which is ____?"

We have been leading a church since we were 25 years old. Many of the people we have ever been blessed to pastor were young and often new Christians. Like new Christians do, these people have had a lot of questions over the years about what is acceptable and unacceptable Christian belief and behavior. One of the most memorable counseling sessions of all time was when we were still a young married couple ourselves, in our mid-20s, and a newly converted couple asked for a meeting to have their questions answered. Usually, the list is fairly predictable—things like creation versus evolution, evidence for

Jesus' resurrection, and proofs for why the Bible is truly God's perfect Word. But this young couple had a vastly different list. She pulled out a spiral bound notebook and started asking the exceptionally lengthy list of many pages of questions they had, to which they simply wanted yes or no answers. "Can we have oral sex?" "Can we have anal sex?" Can we have sex on her period?" Every question was pretty much a different version of the same original question. Thankfully, there are some helpful resources for this kind of research, such as the book, *A Celebration of Sex: A Guide to Enjoying God's Gift of Sexual Intimacy,* by Douglas Rosenau. Not aware of this kind of resource being available so many years ago, I took the couple to a section of Scripture that, in context, is Paul giving categories to the new Christians in Corinth who had come from very sexually promiscuous back-grounds and had a lot of questions. Rather than answering every question, he gives them three questions to consider that will lead them down the path of wisdom and prudence. We will use those same categories to help you as a couple decide what you can and cannot do sexually:

> You say, "I am allowed to do anything"—but not every-thing is good for you. And even though "I am allowed to do anything," I must not become a slave to anything (1 Corinthians 6:12 NLT).

From this Scripture that is speaking about sex, there are three helpful questions for you each to ask when considering sexual acts that you want to try. Each question keeps in focus your relational priorities with God, your spouse, and yourself. These questions are helpful for the more specific and intimate questions that couples have about doing "it"—the things about which they are unsure about or even a little embarrassed to ask. Questions would include things like sex toys, sexual positions, sexual talk during sex, and using technology to be intimate when they are away from each other for things like work or military deployment. The Bible does not speak directly to each of these issues but does speak principally and gives us questions to ask so we can talk to the Lord and our spouse and come to an agreed-upon conclusion that is within the limits of Scripture and our consciences.

1. Relationship with God: Is it sinful?

Some people were apparently saying of their sex life, "I am allowed to do anything," which is something naughty people have said every day since. The truth is, some things are illegal with the government, and other things are sinful with God. We cannot do *whatever* we want sexually, no matter how many times we try to convince ourselves otherwise.

Some things are legal with the government but sinful with God. In the Bible, sexual sin includes homosexuality, erotica, bestiality, bisexuality, fornication, friends with benefits, adultery, swinging, prostitution, incest, rape, polygamy, polyandry, sinful lust, pornography, pedophilia, sexually touching someone else (besides your spouse) in any way with or without clothes on, and sexually viewing or talking to someone else including via technology. The Bible often uses the word *porneia,* from which we get our English word "pornography" as a bit of a catch-all category for various sexual sins. The Bible does this because sinners tend to find new ways to sexually sin. God wants us to deal with our hearts honestly because they lead our hands sinfully. Anything outside of one husband with one wife is a sin.

God's divine design for married sex is solely one husband

and one wife. Anyone else involved in any way is sinful and harmful. Since our culture no longer defines marriage as one man and one woman, it won't be long before more than one person can be considered part of a legal marriage. The Bible is clearer on the sin of homosexuality than the sin of polygamy, and so some who profess to be Christians and support same sex marriage will inevitably join the push for plural marriage by saying that some of God's people in the Bible were polygamous. God's people in the Bible do a lot of terrible things, which does not make them a good example. God made marriage for one man and one woman starting with Adam and Eve, and sex is solely for a marriage between one man and one woman.

If what you want to do sexually as a couple does violate this first question, the answer is "no." If what you want to do sexually as a couple does not violate this first question, then you can move on to the second question.

2. Relationship with spouse: Is it helpful?

When Paul says, "not everything is good for you" sexually, he is distinguishing between a sin and harm. Something may not be a sin in your relationship with God, but it might harm your relationship with your spouse. Just because you can do something does not mean you have to do everything God permits. In the same way, there are lots of foods that you and your spouse are free to eat, and some that you choose not to because you do not enjoy them, and they make you sick. Other people can eat those foods without any trouble, but they don't work for you. Your sex life is a bit like your diet.

Earlier in the book we examined the six reasons God gave us the gift of sex for the strengthening of our marriage:

1. Pleasure[55]
2. Children[56]
3. Knowledge[57]
4. Protection[58]
5. Comfort[59]
6. Oneness[60]

If any one of these things is the result of some sexual act in our marriage, then we are free to consider enjoying it.

Regarding **pleasure**, if you want to do something with your spouse and it causes you pleasure without causing them pain, then it's open for consideration. As we have seen throughout the Song of Songs, the subject is sex in marriage, and there is no mention of children as it's just for the pleasure.

Regarding **children**, if you want to be together strategically at the time you are most likely to conceive because you want kids, then that's great. Children are a blessing, and God chose to bring life into existence at the moment of deepest connection between you and your spouse, which is a beautiful thing and helps fulfill God's command for married couples to "be fruitful and multiply."[61]

Regarding **knowledge**, if you like to do something together because you've never done it with anyone else, it makes you know one another in a more private and intimate way, and you both like it, then consider it. This is what

---

55 Song of Songs
56 Genesis 1:28
57 Genesis 4:1
58 1 Corinthians 7:2–5
59 2 Samuel 12:24
60 Genesis 2:24
61 Genesis 1:28

happened when "Adam knew his wife" as they were enjoying marital sex.[62]

Regarding **protection**, if being sexually active with a certain frequency or freedom keeps the temptation to lust or sin down, then be open to it. Couples often disagree about how often they should have sex and what is a healthy number of times a week. First Corinthians 7:1–5 says,

> Now concerning the matters about which you wrote: "It is good for a man not to have sexual relations with a woman." But because of the temptation to sexual immorality, each man should have his own wife and each woman her own husband. The husband should give to his wife her conjugal rights, and likewise the wife to her husband. For the wife does not have authority over her own body, but the husband does. Likewise the husband does not have authority over his own body, but the wife does. Do not deprive one another, except perhaps by agreement for a limited time, that you may devote yourselves to prayer; but then come together again, so that Satan may not tempt you because of your lack of self-control (ESV).

As servant-lovers, sometimes you serve your spouse by having sex when they want to and you don't want to. Other times, you serve your spouse by not having sex because they don't want to. Sometimes servant-lovers serve by having sex, and sometimes they serve by not having sex.

The Bible gives no number for a healthy frequency, and after reading the entire book of Numbers, sadly we could not find

---

62 Genesis 4:1

that number anywhere. Statistically, the average couple has sex two to four times a week, and many masturbate (often to pornography) additional times that are secrets unknown to their spouses. The couple who has no sinful secrets and only has sex together might logically have it more often than other marriages do. Additionally, as a couple ages, sexual frequency generally goes down for many couples. There are also seasons where normal sexual relations cannot occur (e.g., major illness or injury, recent birth of a child, long military deployment, etc.), which require that a couple have a loving, kind, and reasonable conversation about how they can serve each other in creative ways for that season. The goal is always oneness—to build your life in the bedroom as lovers and outside the bedroom as friends.

> ## THE GOAL IS ALWAYS ONENESS—TO BUILD YOUR LIFE IN THE BEDROOM AS LOVERS AND OUTSIDE THE BEDROOM AS FRIENDS.

Regarding **comfort**, if sometimes you need to be together just not to feel alone and take the edge off a rough day or season, then it can build your marriage. Comfort really does happen when we are physically close with our spouses. When our skin touches each other, our bodies release hormones and other chemicals that comfort us. Researchers contrast this "compassionate love" that is about connecting, with "passionate love" that is about climax.[xxxix] This is precisely how Solomon, the author of Song of Songs and husband to Abishag, was conceived. Second Samuel 12:24 says that after the loss of their first child, "David comforted his wife Bathsheba, and he went to her and made love to her. She gave birth to a son, and they named him Solomon."

Regarding **oneness**, whatever you do, do it together so that there are no shameful sexual secrets in your marriage. Be unified, in agreement, and enjoying sex together as "one flesh" like God intended you to be.[63] The key is to decide as a couple what you want to plant in your marriage garden, because it is something you enjoy.

No matter what, the surest way to make your sexual decisions unhelpful is to share them with other people. We live in a day that has no respect for privacy, and people share the tawdry details of their sex lives in casual conversations and even online. Once again, your marriage is a private garden, not a public park. Other people have no right to peer into your garden or walk around giving their opinion on what you have and have not planted sexually. The only people you should discuss anything private with are agreed upon wise counsel, which is usually best with a pastor, Christian counselor, or godly confidential mentor who, your spouse agrees should be spoken to for advice on intimate issues.

If what you want to do will build and not break your marriage, honor and not dishonor both of your consciences, and make you both feel cared for and not used or abused, then you can consider that possible sexual act in light of the third and last question.

3. Relationship with self: Is it addictive?

The Holy Spirit through Paul says, "Even though 'I am allowed to do anything,' I must not become a slave to anything" (1 Corinthians 6:12 NLT). There are a lot of things in life that are not bad in moderation but become a real problem when

---

63 Genesis 2:24

combined with addiction. For example, a beer is no problem if you are an adult who drinks one, but beer becomes a real problem when you drink a case with every meal. The same is true with food and why eating a scoop of ice cream once in a while is fine, but indulging in gallons every night is slow suicide.

When the Bible uses the word "slave," it speaks of the bondage of addiction. A slave is the person who has someone or something ruling over them so they are not free to live as God wants. A slave master is a brutal tyrant who pushes the slave until they break and eventually die.

Often, the master that enslaves us is not an evil thing but rather something that can be good or bad depending upon whether we rule over it or it rules over us. Something may not be sinful, but if it harms our relationship with God or our spouse, violates a conscience, or begins to replace normal, regular marital sexual intimacy, then it could be displacing a healthy marital relationship.

The field of brain science is still emerging, but it is already revealing some incredible facts about how God actually hard-wired our brains for chastity before marriage and fidelity in marriage. The passions and pleasures of nudity and sex release dopamine in the brain's pleasure center, which can be used to either bond us with our spouse or with someone or something else through practices such as adultery or pornography. Researchers at Harvard report, "Being love-struck also releases high levels of dopamine, a chemical that 'gets the reward system going'... Dopamine activates the reward circuit, helping to make love a pleasurable experience similar to the euphoria associated with use of cocaine or alcohol."[xl]

Orgasms trigger oxytocin and vasopressin, which create attachment and bonding. Scientific American says, "If cupid had studied neuroscience, he'd know to aim his arrows at the brain rather than the heart. Recent research suggests that for love to last, it's best he dips those arrows in oxytocin."[xli] Researchers at Harvard say, "Released during sex and heightened by skin-to-skin contact, oxytocin deepens feelings of attachment and makes couples feel closer to one another after having sex. Oxytocin, known also as the love hormone, provokes feelings of contentment, calmness, and security, which are often associated with mate bonding. Vasopressin is linked to behavior that produces long-term, monogamous relationships."[xlii] As we repeatedly experience sexual pleasure from the same source, habitual neural pathways are created in the brain that make it faster and easier for us to achieve pleasure and the climax of orgasm. God created all of this so we would bond with and be devoted to our spouse and invest our lives in our marriages. Everything God creates Satan counterfeits, and when it comes to habituating and hardwiring our brain for marriage, he hijacks it for sin and sexual addiction. Satan does not care what sexual sin we choose (pornography, adultery, sinful fantasy, etc.), because when combined with the rush of knowing we are disobeying (or are at risk of getting caught), the overwhelming attachment to whatever provides the pleasure leads to habits and addictions. This fact explains why some people have odd sexual fetishes, and others cannot enjoy healthy married sex—they have so bonded with someone or something other than their spouse that they would rather run down old neural pleasure pathways to sin and death than build new neural pleasure pathways to marriage and life.

The good news is we can build new neural pathways and overcome bad behaviors and even addictions. The key is to be intentional and mindful. Refer to "taking every thought captive" in the previous chapter. This is precisely the issue the Holy Spirit's third question through the apostle Paul is requiring you and your spouse to discuss prayerfully and humbly whatever sexual activity you want to try together. The same God who created your bodies, made you male and female, designed sex, and invented marriage also wrote the Bible as a diagnostic tool to help you love God and your spouse with all your heart (emotional life), soul (spiritual life), mind (mental life), and strength (physical life).

Practically, this may mean that one couple can use sex toys, but another cannot because it leads to an addiction where they no longer desire being with their spouse and instead are frequently using the toys without their spouse knowing, not promoting oneness. One couple may be fine using technology to see one another sexually while they are apart (e.g., long business trip or military deployment), but another couple cannot because it triggers an old addiction cycle that leads to watching pornography of other people and sinful lust. This final question requires some real honest searching of ourselves and sharing with our spouse, which is the next assignment.

FACE-TO-FACE QUESTIONS
for Couple Discussion

First, before you meet, take some time to individually think through what things you are doing in your sex life together that may not meet the criteria of the three questions and make a list of anything you need to discuss with your spouse. Second, before you meet, take some time to also think through what new thing(s) you would like to possibly try and consider them through the three questions. Then, meet with your spouse, open in prayer, and share your thoughts based upon this chapter. Decide what changes need to be made in terms of stopping some sexual acts and starting (or at least trying) new ones. Lastly, end the private conversation by sharing what your favorite sexual memories are together and why.

Chapter 8

TO THE COUNTRYSIDE
7:11–8:7

She

7:11 Come, my beloved, let us go to the countryside,
let us spend the night in the villages.

12 Let us go early to the vineyards
to see if the vines have budded,
if their blossoms have opened,
and if the pomegranates are in bloom—
there I will give you my love.

13 The mandrakes send out their fragrance,
and at our door is every delicacy,
both new and old,
that I have stored up for you, my beloved.

8:1 If only you were to me like a brother,
who was nursed at my mother's breasts!
Then, if I found you outside,
I would kiss you,
and no one would despise me.

2 I would lead you
and bring you to my mother's house—
she who has taught me.
I would give you spiced wine to drink,
the nectar of my pomegranates.
3 His left arm is under my head
and his right arm embraces me.
4 Daughters of Jerusalem, I charge you:
Do not arouse or awaken love
until it so desires.

Friends

5 Who is this coming up from the wilderness
leaning on her beloved?

She

Under the apple tree I roused you;
There your mother conceived you,
there she who was in labor gave you birth.
6 Place me like a seal over your heart,
like a seal on your arm;
for love is as strong as death,
its jealousy unyielding as the grave.
It burns like blazing fire,
like a mighty flame.
7 Many waters cannot quench love;
rivers cannot sweep it away.
If one were to give
all the wealth of one's house for love,
it would be utterly scorned.

———

When we first married, we got into a bad habit of not getting a weekly Sabbath day off or planning for holidays and vacations. We had "good" reasons to justify our overwork. In college, we were very broke, and since we were paying our way through college, we worked as much as we could to avoid debt. We hoped things would settle into a better routine once we were graduated, but the opposite happened. At first, Grace worked nights, and I worked days, and we did not have the same days off as we were housesitting from place to place trying to save enough money to get into an apartment. Eventually, Grace was able to get a job with normal hours, but things only got worse once we started leading a college ministry. We both worked all day and had Bible studies and college students in our house most nights. Then the college ministry morphed into a church plant we founded and volunteered at for the first three years, working additional jobs to fund the struggling little church. Once Grace got pregnant with our first child, she quit her good-paying corporate job doing advertising, and I started writing, speaking, and traveling in addition to pastoring to provide for our growing family and church family.

Our sin was not one of commission—we were not doing anything "sinful"—as everything we were doing was for the Lord. Our sin was one of omission—we were not getting a Sabbath. Three things happened.

First, our holidays were not architected for life and memories. Our worst holiday was our first Christmas after college graduation. We were both working long hours and wrongly assumed that the other person would make holiday plans. We both got home late on Christmas Eve, and our families, whom we usually spent the day with, had left town a day early. We were both crushed once we realized we had nothing in our rental home that looked like Christmas; there was zero evidence of any holiday. We did not get a tree, stockings, décor, or any wrapped gifts. We were so busy serving everyone else that we missed our own marriage. We tried to go out to dinner, but the restaurants were closed. This left us at home eating the only thing left in the kitchen—pancakes—as the refrigerator was empty since we were leaving town the next day. For the record, I (Mark) do not like pancakes very much. Spiraling toward depression for our failure, we headed to see a movie that looked like it would be romantic. But halfway through "Bridges of Madison County," we realized it was a film about adultery, so we left early and just went to bed.

Second, our vacations were not architected for rest and joy. With little kids and no money, we struggled to figure out how to get the time off work and also to find a place we could afford where the entire family could have fun and make memories. On a few occasions, well-intended people in the church offered their "free" cabins. I learned the hard way that you get what you pay for and that dad should always go investigate any potential family vacation spot in advance. After loading up the kids, and all their stuff, including their bikes so that our Suburban looked like it was the rolling residence of a hoarder, we pulled up to the cabin, only to find it had a cat and a broken and extremely dangerous deck. Our daughter is very allergic to cats, and her eyes pretty much swelled shut as she struggled to breathe. Our son kept wanting to go play on the deck with a broken railing and missing floor planks. The cabin also had an extremely large buffalo head on the wall that horrified the kids. So we turned around, went home, and I went back to work.

Third, if you don't take a break, then you will break. Grace has always been better at managing her wellness, and I tend just to keep working until I cannot work anymore. Grace works very, very hard and gets a ton done. She has proven throughout our marriage to be better at self-care and health than me. Twice I have completely fried my adrenal glands and neurotransmitters, and in too many seasons, rather than taking a break, I simply broke.

We wish we could say we learned our lessons quickly and adjusted early, but that would not be true. Three things have helped, though. First, we have spent a lot of time studying the concept of Sabbath in the Bible, which we will share with you in this chapter. Second, we have a shared digital calendar so we can organize our life as "one" with everything from the kids' school and sports, to breaks and holidays, birthdays, vacations, and work commitments. Third, we have a weekly calendar meeting where we go through the upcoming week, month, and year in detail to carve our time for Sabbaths and holidays, which also allows us to pace our work and prepare our budget. We always try to have fun on the calendar, even if it's simple—something to look forward to where we can get out of our work routine, make memories, take photos, and enjoy each other and the life God has given us. Without fun on the calendar, life can get dark and daunting very quickly.

Keep Dating After You Are Married

Prior to marriage, a couple spends a lot of their time and energy planning for and making memories on fun dates. We open our schedules, make plans, and intentionally make memories and have fun together, which helps us fall in love. Too often, though, we get married and become so busy with our responsibilities that we neglect our romance and stop dating.

This rut is precisely where we find ourselves in the story of the Song of Songs. Having been married a while, Solomon has grown increasingly busy at work, and Abbi is longing to get some time away together. When she says she wishes he were like a brother, it means she is tired of being public figures with royal roles and responsibilities. In that culture, public displays of affection were frowned upon, and because Solomon was King of Israel, she did not get to hold his hand, give him a kiss, or snuggle up, because they were almost always together at formal work events for the nation. In that culture, when kids were little, however, it was acceptable for a little brother and sister to hold hands, give each other a peck on the cheek, or sit closely together. Abbi she wants to have more private time and less public time to do those very things. Imagine living where you work, complete with 24-hour staff, security guards, assistants, visiting guests, and constant emergencies. If you have a high-stress job, live a life that is more public than private, are in a very professional career, or have to travel a lot for work, then you understand the struggle that this section of Song of Songs explains.

Abbi and Solomon, like most couples, are willing to get time together, but life has crept in making them unable to do so. If you are reading this book, then odds are you want to get more time and connection with your spouse, but the demands of life have crowded out the desires of love. The key is to take your life back and get your love back, just as Abbi models for us.

Rather than nagging her husband, Abbi invites him to come away with her to a private romantic break in the countryside. She does not want anything on their schedule, probably because their life is already too scheduled. She wants to wake up whenever they feel like it and do whatever they feel like doing throughout each day of their break. She also mentions that it is springtime—the time when nature and love tend to bloom and a wonderful time to go to a quiet, out-of-the-way place. Her flirtation seems to also promise the risqué proposition of making love outside in the countryside, something impossible in their normal life but definitely worth looking forward to and imagining as their time away approached. In this scene, Abbi is building anticipation and imagination, which help draw the couple together, build their intimacy heading into lovemaking, and keep the relationship fun, playful, and adventurous. If you are a bit shy, struggle with being sexually creative, or wonder what is acceptable and unacceptable for a Christian couple, Douglas Rosenau's book *A Celebration of Sex,* which we mentioned earlier, might be a useful resource. If you're needing to work through sexual issues, Dave and Ashley Willis's *The Counterfeit Climax* is also helpful.

Abbi encourages Solomon to make their time away a priority and reminds him of the fun romantic memories they made before they were married. In talking about her mothers' house, she reminds him of the many times he came to court her at her home. She also mentions the "apple tree," which is where they would sit in its shade to visit and fall in love. Curiously, the couple in the Song of Songs is not the only one to sing about falling in love under an apple tree, as the famous old love song called "Don't Sit Under the Apple Tree" warns.

It is important for every couple to look back at the good times they have had and look forward to the good times they

> **IT IS IMPORTANT FOR EVERY COUPLE TO LOOK BACK AT THE GOOD TIMES THEY HAVE HAD AND LOOK FORWARD TO THE GOOD TIMES THEY WILL HAVE.**

will have. As Abbi recalls her favorite memories of their days gazing into one another's eyes and falling in love, it should remind us to take time now and then as a couple to look through old photos, read old letters, watch old videos, and pull out the heartfelt keepsakes we kept from the early years of our blossoming romance. If you're still in the early years, keep those letters and photos in a special, sacred place so you can pull them out to refresh yourselves on why and how you fell in love. Reminisce on your anniversary or Valentine's Day so you can keep the romance going.

To create anticipation for their time, rather than criticizing Solomon for their lack of time together away, Abbi coyly welcomes him to enjoy some of their favorite "old" sexual activities, as well as some "new" things she's wanted to try sexually but has not yet had the courage to initiate. In this, we see the simple principle that holds true: sometimes we get into a rut in our life and sex life, and by getting away to a new place with a free schedule, it helps the couple (especially the wife) to focus on the relationship and be present for flirtation, foreplay, and frolicking in a way that is more difficult when she is at home surrounded by kids and chores.

I (Grace) am a worker bee who likes to stay focused on getting my tasks done while I'm home. With five kids and always something to clean, cook, or take care of, I must diligently refocus on tending to my marriage relationship as a priority rather than going on autopilot. If I'm home, I hear the laundry or kitchen calling me, so it's helpful for me to change my environment to focus solely on Mark and building our marriage in new and fun ways. We generally plan times on the calendar to take a day trip or even a few hours away to laugh and make memories. One time I surprised Mark and planned a fun spa day (Groupon has great deals) that included uninterrupted massages and hanging out by the pool to relax, talk, and laugh. Then we concluded our date at home that evening after the kids were in bed. It takes creativity and planning but doesn't have to be elaborate or expensive. Heading to the beach, going on a hike, camping (not for me, but you are welcome to), or going into the countryside like they did in Song of Songs can be a fabulous change of scenery and allow fresh ideas as you enjoy fresh air.

In particular, Abbi tells Solomon that she wants his left arm under her head, and his right arm embracing her. Once again, we see that this wife is free and frank—she knows what she likes, and she tells her man. Here, she is explaining to him exactly how she wants to be held, including heavy petting and caressing in preparation for lovemaking. Ladies, the truth is most guys do not know what they are doing when it comes to lovemaking, and a bit of coaching along the way is always appreciated. Any guy who played sports growing up will tell you that a good coach is a significant help, and since sex is likely your husband's all-time favorite sport, we'd encourage you to be his coach. One Bible commentator says she "imagines Solomon's left hand under her head as she lies on her back, and his right hand 'embracing' or 'fondling' her breasts and 'garden.'"[xliii]

The entire point of this section and the entirety of this series of romantic snapshots is their "love." In this section, we *learn seven truths about love* that are good points on which to ponder in our own heart about our God, spouse, and marriage covenant.

1. **Love is personal.** When they speak of a seal on their heart, they are talking in very personal terms. In that day, a seal was a bit like a notary or signed legal document in our day, and it was used to conduct business

and confer ownership. If you put your seal on something (e.g., a legal document or the Roman seal that was affixed to the tomb of Jesus), then you are declaring it to be your possession and yours alone. Their love is personal in that they belong to one another, and the seal on their hearts belongs to their beloved alone.

2. **Love is passionate.** When Song of Songs speaks of their love as a "flame," we are encouraged to remember the hot passion of love and lovemaking. Many couples illustrate this very thing during their wedding ceremony when they each have a candle and together light a unity candle showing that God has lit their flame of passion for one another, and their passion will unite as a singular burning and dancing hot flame.

3. **Love is protective.** When Song of Songs speaks of the "arm," it is denoting the strength of defense. Satan and evildoers are always attacking the marriage, so it must be defended and protected. As we have stated, Satan did not even begin his attack until Adam and Eve were married because he hates love and marriage. To protect your marriage, you must "arm" yourselves with the spiritual armor Paul writes about in Ephesians 6 that is preceded by his discussion of marriage in Ephesians 5. Arm your marriage for spiritual warfare.

4. **Love is powerful.** Death is always victorious and permanent. Love, however, is more powerful than death as it defeats death and outlives life. For example, Jesus' love for us defeated death and is permanent for God's people. It is that same love that God gives us from the

Holy Spirit to flow through us to our spouse to live by the supreme power of supernatural love.

5. **Love is possessive.** We often think of "jealousy" as being negative, but here it is positive and the result of healthy love. Godly jealousy happens when someone we love has given our place in their life to another. This explains why God is a jealous God.[64] God is like a husband, and His people are like His bride in a common metaphor used throughout the Bible. God gets jealous when someone or something takes His place, and the same is true for a loving, healthy couple.

6. **Love is priceless.** When they say love is something you cannot buy with "wealth," the couple is referring to the fact that, unlike goods and services, love is something that another person must give—we cannot take or purchase it. You can buy time from a therapist to speak with you, and you can buy service from an employee to care for you, but you cannot buy love. Love is not cheap; it is priceless, which is why it has no price.

7. **Love perseveres.** When they say that you "cannot quench love" nor "sweep it away," the big idea is that when earthquakes shake life, floods overwhelm life, hurricanes upend life, and fires consume life, the one thing that will remain is love. The sociologists tell us most couples who divorce do so by the eighth year, as the seven-year itch is apparently a real thing. Furthermore, the experts tell us that it takes between 9 and 14 years for a person to become unselfish and

---

64 Exodus 20:4–6; Deuteronomy 4:24

care more about "we" than "me." The more you persevere in your marriage, the more you learn not to use
your spouse for what you want but to love your spouse
as God loves you.

Having spent 30 years together faithfully married as we
write this book, we can testify to this fact. Love that is personal, passionate, protective, powerful, possessive, and priceless does persevere. Over the years we have lost friends, jobs,
houses, and much more, but we have not lost our love for one
another. We want the same for you, which is why we want to
help you make your love a priority. In order to keep dating
while you are married, it's good to have date nights, sabbaths,
vacations, and holidays. We will study each of these next.

> **LOVE THAT IS PERSONAL, PASSIONATE,
> PROTECTIVE, POWERFUL, POSSESSIVE,
> AND PRICELESS DOES PERSEVERE.**

Date Night

In talking about Abbi's longing to get a break from life's rou-
tines and work, it seems like they have not had a regular date
night. To be sure, every couple needs Sabbath breaks, some
vacations, and getaways, but when we have neglected a regular weekly time together, things become more urgent.

One piece of great advice our pastor gave us during our
premarital counseling was the importance of a weekly date.
This could be a date day, date night, or even a date that lasts

both day and night. We started this ritual in college and have kept it throughout our married life.

This habit has been vital for us to have a time to count on each week and a good example for other couples as we held it sacred and didn't schedule anything else in that time slot. Since we've been together in dating and marriage for over 30 years, the day itself has varied each week, but we always put it on the schedule first and plan other things around it. Whether I (Grace) was working outside or inside the home, it was helpful to know that we could connect more deeply than "How was your day?" or "Did you pick up the kids?" at least once a week in our date time together. It was a time to pause from the normal busyness and look each other in the eye. We could encourage one another, talk about relational issues that came up during the week, and really listen to how each of us was doing. Enjoying our dates was what drew us together in the first place, and if we wanted to continue to grow our marriage, it was necessary to get intentional time to connect. Ladies, we are usually great at doing this with female friendships, but it is even more important to invest this time in our marriages. As a side note, if you have girlfriends who don't help you build your marriage (Abbi had good friends), then you need to consider if they should be your friends. Anyone who is pulling your marriage down or demanding to be priority over your husband is not a good friend.

As poor college newlyweds, we had to get creative with our dates. We had a lot of picnics at the park, and we would go for adventurous drives to find fun spots to hike or watch the sunset. We might eat dinner at home but go out for fun dessert, and we found other creative ways to have fun without spending a lot of money. These dates include playing board games, which Grace likes (Mark calls them "bored games"), or sitting at a coffee shop to chat or play cards.

If you are prioritizing marriage, then you will take money and time to invest in it. We made our coffee at home, brought lunch to work, pinched pennies where we could, and prayed for God's provision to build our marriage. We worked hard and tithed firstfruits to the Lord, but honestly, looking back, it doesn't even make sense how we were able to do the things we did with five kids living in an awfully expensive city. Only God showing up and blessing us explains how we got to travel, enjoy getaways, and be generous with others. God wants to honor and bless our marriage when we make it a priority. Everything else is working against us, so spend time together asking God to show you how to enjoy each other and be unified.

As our kids were born, we were blessed to have both sets of grandparents living nearby, They took turns on Friday nights watching the children so we could get a date. Friends of ours who did not have safe relatives nearby would often form a dating co-op where four to six couples would take turns watching everyone's kids once every four to six weeks, and then enjoy a date night with free childcare on the other weeks.

Creativity does not need to come with high expense. Some couples prefer having a massage table in their bedroom to give each other restful, erotic massages. Some couples like to take turns being blindfolded in the bedroom for date nights and let their spouse surprise them with what happens next. Some couples spend date night naked and sleep in the nude one night a week, which is fun and cuts down on laundry. One couple nicknamed the first year of their date nights "Freaky Friday," and the only rule was they had to try something new sexually to see if they like it. You can even sit in the tub with a glass of wine, read the Song of Songs to each other, and then

> **SPEND TIME TOGETHER ASKING GOD TO SHOW YOU HOW TO ENJOY EACH OTHER AND BE UNIFIED.**

make love so that you are not merely hearers of the Word but doers, as James exhorts. The key is to get out of your menial rut and get into a freer mindset.

Some couples like to go camping, which is an inexpensive way to have a getaway. Grace, however, is a lot more like Ginger than MaryAnn if you are familiar with the old television show "Gilligan's Island," The odds of getting her to go camping are about the same as getting me to conceive a child, so we've never camped. Grace does, however, have some friends who like glamping. Their tents include nice beds, chandeliers, and a lot of princess amenities. Whatever works for you is great.

With little kids and a new church plant, money was tight, so we started asking friends and family to give us gift cards for movies and meals for our birthdays and holidays. These were tremendous blessings that allowed us some nice evenings we otherwise could not afford. Later, we started putting expenses on a credit card we paid off every month so we could garner points to later use for an overnight date at a hotel, special dinner, or even flights to special destinations.

Some couples will even fly in a grandparent to stay with the kids for a few nights so they can get away for a romantic and restful time. These times build your marriage relationship as well as a connection between your children and their grandparent, so everyone is blessed.

Our intent in this chapter is to get you to plan creatively and prepare for an ongoing dating relationship that never ends. This includes learning to Sabbath together.

Sabbaths

Many couples include their weekly date as part of their weekly Sabbath. In the opening chapters of Genesis, God created a seven-day week by working six days and resting on the seventh. The Hebrew language, in which Genesis was originally written, that God breathed out for six days, and on the seventh day He breathed in. Overworked and overwhelmed people who say something such as, "I need to take a break and catch my breath" are agreeing with God.

Curiously, people who hate God have tried to have societies built on something other than a seven-day week. During the French Revolution led by Napoleon (1793–1805), a failed attempt was made to have a 10-day week. Under Joseph Stalin (1929–1940), the Russians unsuccessfully sought to end the worship of God on a Sabbath day by eliminating weekends and having a complicated "continuous week" with various people groups given various and seemingly random intermittent days off.

The original recipients of Genesis were Hebrew slaves who had been forced to work seven days a week in Egypt before God delivered them to worship Him on a Sabbath day of rest for replenishment and recovery. God gave the Sabbath to them in the Ten Commandments.[65] Solomon and Abbi were Jewish, so they were very familiar with the Jewish protocols, which involved working six days a week and taking a day off as God had modeled.

Saturday was kept by God's people as the Sabbath until the Resurrection of Jesus Christ on a Sunday, or what John in Revelation calls "the Lord's Day."[66] Jesus taught that the

---

65 Exodus 20:8–11
66 Revelation 1:10

Sabbath was a grace to serve us, not a law to rule over us.[67] The New Testament says we should have a Sabbath day, but we get to pick what day that is. Romans 14:5–6 says, "One person esteems one day as better than another, while another esteems all days alike. Each one should be fully convinced in his own mind. The one who observes the day, observes it in honor of the Lord."

When it came to deciding which day Americans would Sabbath, there was a debate between the Jewish Sabbath of Saturday and the more common Christian Sabbath of Sunday in honor of Jesus' resurrection. The compromise was made that we would get both days, which is how the U.S. came to have a five-day week and two-day weekend.

On your Sabbath day, you should do whatever you find restful, replenishing, and refreshing. If gardening, hiking, cycling, napping, beachcombing, off-roading, reading, wood-working, painting, songwriting, movie-watching, cooking, grilling, baking, boating, swimming, spa lounging, body massaging, car restoring, bonfire watching, knitting, quilt-ing, or gardening put life in you, then do it on your day off.

Learning to Sabbath together can be difficult for many cou-ples. We rest and recover very differently. I (Mark) am more of an introvert—I like to stay up late and sleep in, and I prefer to be outdoors whenever possible (especially eating dinner outside watching the sunset). I am very spatially aware and do not like to be in an environment that is dirty, cluttered, disorganized, loud, or poorly designed. The environment I am in matters a great deal to me and helps me wind down and relax. On the other hand, I (Grace) can be in any space and be content, as long as it's quiet. This was more challenging with all the kids at home but not an excuse to ignore Sabbath. When they napped

---

67 Mark 2:27

or had quiet time in their rooms, I had to build the habit of taking some of that time to rest so I could have something to invest again. If we are only pouring out but not getting time for the Holy Spirit to pour into us, we will burn out or not be doing our responsibilities to the best of our abilities. Technology is also a major distraction to Sabbath, so I would encourage you to put it away in order to focus on rest and time with the Lord.

> **IF WE ARE ONLY POURING OUT BUT NOT GETTING TIME FOR THE HOLY SPIRIT TO POUR INTO US, WE WILL BURN OUT OR NOT BE DOING OUR RESPONSIBILITIES TO THE BEST OF OUR ABILITIES.**

A couple who learns to Sabbath together one day a week is best prepared to plan and execute extended vacation times together. Sadly, some couples report their vacation time is spent arguing, frustrated, disappointed, or stressed, and God desires the exact opposite, which is why it is important to pray and plan your vacations together.

Vacations

Planning a good vacation takes a lot of praying and preparing. The time leading up to a vacation is usually incredibly stressful, as all the work and chores need to be done prior to leaving for a break. Since sin entered the world and brought with it the Fall and curse, everything is prone to fall apart rather than come together, and this is doubly true with vacations. As the old adage goes, "If you fail to plan, then you plan to fail."

The earlier you start planning your vacation, the better the odds it will be a blessing and not a curse. As a couple, you need to have many discussions about what does and does not work for you on vacation. If you have children, it's good to plan some getaways throughout the year without the kids, as well as family vacations, which are wonderfully fun but also exhausting and not very restful.

- Where will we go? Will we drive or fly?

- Where will we stay? Do we want to camp, stay in a rental home, or go to a hotel?

- What will we pack? How much packing is overpacking?

- How will we eat—grocery shopping and cooking like at home or eating out and takeout?

- What will we do with our technology? Will we keep our phones on or off? Will we be doing no work or allow work to creep in on our vacation?

- How much will we plan? Will we fill every day with a detailed itinerary, plan just one outing per day and leave the rest of the time flexible, or have no schedule at all and take it one day at a time?

- Are there any special needs we have? If we bring the kids, are they safe, and can they make noise without getting us in trouble? Are the beds comfortable so we can all sleep?

These are just a few sample questions of the kinds of discussions that go into planning a fantastic vacation. We were not good at this when we were first married, but thankfully we have gotten much better. We now have wonderful memories as a couple and as a family with our kids going on fun adventures big and small across town and across the globe. We have tens of thousands of fun photos and videos capturing these sacred moments. We have fun reviewing them now and then to remember the fun times and laughs, and then we thank God for His grace with which He has saturated our lives.

For planning family vacations when the kids were little, we would hold family meetings where we'd hear what they wanted to do and consider what would be fun for everyone. We tried to integrate into the planning something fun for everyone. On vacation, we would write or type out the rough daily plan and post it on the fridge so that if we needed to be up at a certain time, or were heading out for an adventure day, the kids knew in advance. We didn't schedule more than one thing a day and tried to keep a lot of margin for sleep and spontaneity. We also included dates when we were not with the kids and got to do some fun romantic things as a couple. We believe it was modeling for the children at an early age the importance of marriage and keeping your spouse as your priority as part of their discipleship.

The key to an ever-improving marriage it to become a student of your spouse. Keep learning about who they are and what they like and keep working to improve how you love and serve them. This fact is doubly true when it comes to planning vacations. It is wise to keep a journal or file with all the things that work and don't work on your vacations and holidays so you can keep improving your special and sacred times together.

Staycations are becoming increasingly popular for some couples. We are often so busy with work and life that we do not take the time to enjoy the sites within driving distance of our homes. A couple disciplined enough to turn their phones and work life off could schedule a series of day trips to go explore where they live while coming back to sleep in the comfort of their own bed. If you have little kids, this can be a lot easier than a cross-country trip with time changes and new surroundings *if* you are disciplined enough to rest and not fall back into old patterns of doing the chores and catching up on work from the office while at home.

Some couples house swap with friends for vacations. If you've got family or friends with a house and a car somewhere you would like to vacation, maybe they would trade with you so you could both get a nice break at an inexpensive price point.

Rather than spending money on vacations, some couples decide to invest that money in their home so they can enjoy a series of staycations. Such things as outdoor dining spaces, outdoor firepits, swimming pools, hot tubs, or romantic private bedrooms and bathrooms for the couple can all be used year-round to rest and recover at home whenever you want.

Other couples who can afford it save up to buy, or purchase with other family or friends, a vacation property within a few hours driving distance of their home. Renting it out when it's not in use can also help cover the expense, and having a regular place that is known and has your amenities can be an incredible way to get regular vacations as a couple and family.

Holidays

One of the most important truths a married couple needs to acknowledge, and their extended family needs to accept, is that they are a new and separate family. When a couple is married, her side often talks about how excited they are to have a son join their family, and his side talks about how excited they are to have a daughter join their family.

These sentiments are often well-intended but completely misguided. When the Bible says that a man should leave his parents and pursue his wife, it is so they can start their own family. When I (Mark) officiated the weddings of our oldest son and daughter (our younger children are unmarried as we write this), I was clear to everyone in my sermon that the newly married couple was starting their own new family, and they had the right to decide how they would live their life, enjoy their holidays, spend their money, take their vacations, and raise their children.

Before our children were married, they were part of our family. Once our children are married, they are their own family. We become their extended family, and because we are no longer their priority, we should work around them and not demand that they work around us. For example, before our oldest daughter was married, I (Mark) was the main man in her life. I helped her make all her decisions, and she spent her holidays and vacations with us. I loved every single minute of this season of our life, but that season is over. Today, her husband is the main man in her life. He gets to make decisions with her, plan vacations with her, and enjoy the holidays with her. My goal is to do all I can to help them have a healthy, loving, joyful, and God-centered marriage, and I must accept that my role has changed. We have wonderful and close relationships with our grown children, see them all the time, have big, bi-weekly family dinners, and enjoy some holidays and vacations together, *but* none of this is demanded or required. Everything is open-handed, and we do not take offense if our grown, married children do things as a couple that do not involve us. Our house, schedule, and budget are open to them, and we expect nothing in return. Our goal is to give and not take, bless and not burden, help and not hinder their family.

Holidays can be a very tough time on a marriage. These days often take money out of the budget and time off the calendar, which can cause stress. Dysfunctional families who do not enjoy a healthy relationship throughout the year commonly put a lot of pressure on every member of the family to be together and give the false impression that they are one big happy family. Healthy families make memories and enjoy time throughout the year so that the holidays are not so pressure-packed with high emotions and expectations.

Once all our five children marry, we will have six families and not one. Grace and I will be a family, just like we were before our kids were born. Each of our children and their spouses (and kids) will be their own families. Each family has the right and responsibility to decide what they want to do for vacations and holidays and should have the freedom to make those decisions every year, based upon whatever factors they deem important without feeling obligated. The parents should have the freedom to make their own family holiday traditions. If the grandparents or other extended family members want to offer or suggest some holiday festivities to do together as extended families, then that is wonderful, but it should be an invitation and not a demand. The Bible has a lot to say about the difference between grace and law. Sometimes the worst laws come from the in-laws. When parents and extended family members press too hard and demand too much, it can cause a lot of conflict in a marriage between the husband and wife or require that they pull back and create a firm boundary, which causes hurt and distance that should not be necessary if things are healthy and godly.

As a coaching point, most of the time if there is a conversation that needs to be had with extended family members who are unhealthy or unwilling to respect healthy boundaries between families, it is best if each of you speak to your own extended families. If the husband's side is the problem, then he should sketch out with his wife what he will say and be the one to say it. She can be at his side for support if they and wise counsel deem that best, but he should do most of the talking and have the hard conversation. Conversely, if the wife's side is the problem, then they should agree together on what to say, how to say it, when and where to meet (in a safe place), but she should do most of the talking. If we do not have these kinds of clarifying conversations, then things can boil under the surface until they erupt like a volcano, causing a lot of emotion and drama, drawing the extended family into division by taking sides, and creating turmoil. Some family issues feel like a grenade with the pin pulled, so using care and caution with preparation, prayer, and planning is the best way to diffuse what would otherwise eventually blow up.

Hope, Help, Healing

In reading this chapter, it is likely some areas of fault, frustration, and failure became obvious. Do not be discouraged by this fact. In returning to the story of Solomon and Abbi in this chapter, they were in a bad place. He was working too much, they did not get time alone, she was frustrated and lonely, and they were not getting enough Sabbath time, dates, or vacations together. They got it wrong before they got it right, which is the whole message of the entire Bible. Rarely, if ever, does anyone of us get anything right the first time. We learn through trial and error, doing it wrong and then making changes until we get it right. That is the story and testimony of this chapter, our marriage, and every Christian. The following discussion questions are intended to help you sit down to pray for and plan out good times for you and your marriage. God loves you, and the best is yet to come, so be determined and don't get discouraged.

FACE-TO-FACE QUESTIONS
for Couple Discussion

1. After reading this chapter, is there anything you need to own, apologize for, or recognize as unhealthy or unhelpful?

2. Do you have a shared calendar to organize your life together as "one"? How is it going keeping it organized? When is your weekly calendar meeting going to be?

3. When is your weekly date going to be? What two or three things would each of you request to improve your weekly date?

4. When is your weekly Sabbath going to be? What two or three things would each of you request to improve your Sabbath day?

5. When will you set aside two or three hours to discuss the holidays for the next year and how to make them the best you can?

6. When will you set aside two or three hours to discuss and plan vacations, breaks, and getaways to make them as restful and memorable they can be?

Chapter 9

MY OWN VINEYARD
8:8—8:14

Brothers

8:8 We have a little sister,
and her breasts are not yet grown.
What shall we do for our sister
on the day she is spoken for?

9 If she is a wall,
we will build towers of silver on her.
If she is a door,
we will enclose her with panels of cedar.

She

10 I am a wall,
and my breasts are like towers.
Thus I have become in his eyes
like one bringing contentment.

11 Solomon had a vineyard in Baal Hamon;
he let out his vineyard to tenants.
Each was to bring for its fruit
a thousand shekels of silver.

12 But my own vineyard is mine to give;
the thousand shekels are for you, Solomon,
and two hundred are for those who tend its fruit.

He

13 You who dwell in the gardens
with friends in attendance,
let me hear your voice!

She

14 Come away, my beloved,
and be like a gazelle
or like a young stag
on the spice-laden mountains.

———

Because so much of Christianity has spread from the Western world (e.g., Bible translations, global ministry headquarters, Bible colleges and seminaries, missions organizations, etc.), we can easily overlook the simple fact that our faith is largely Eastern. The Hebrew mindset of the Old Testament is different than our English world dominated by Greek thinking and western storytelling.

In the west, we are all familiar with fairytales and love stories that are read to us starting at an early age. The format for a Western story is generally consistent: beginning-middle-end. Most of our stories are told in linear fashion and chronological order. The conclusion of our love stories is often, "And they lived happily ever after." Most of the stories and books of the Bible are not written this way. For example, out of the four Gospels that tell the life story of Jesus Christ, only Luke is written in chronological order.

In the East, the format for a story is often: beginning-middle-beginning. The Bible itself is written in this Eastern format and mindset. The first two chapters of Genesis both repeat the story of the beginning. Genesis 3 introduces Satan, sin, the Fall, and curse. The middle of history is about sin and the Savior. The end of the story is actually a return to the beginning of the story. The first two chapters of Genesis that open the Bible and the last two chapters of Revelation that close the Bible tell the same story. God returns to His original, divinely designed plan and goes back to the beginning with a new beginning. The first two and last two chapters of the Bible show the world without sin, ruled by God, with heaven and earth together, the Tree of Life, humanity in perfection amidst a garden, with flowing water, sunlight, and fruit as God's human family and divine family live together in perfection forever.

When we read the Bible, we can tend to think of God making things new as something completely different from anything He has done before. The truth is, when God finished His work, He said everything was "good" and everyone was "very good," so there was nothing to improve on. God got everything and everyone right and perfect the first time. Our sin has infected and affected everyone and everything, and God renews by removing sin and returning to His original divine design.

The point of Eastern storytelling is that, to have a good ending, you need a good beginning. If you have a bad beginning, then God needs to give you a new beginning so you can have a good ending. This explains why Jesus told Nicodemus we must be born again. To have a good eternal ending after this life, we need a new beginning in this life.

This difference between the Western and Eastern modes

of storytelling explains why Christians in the West have struggled to interpret Song of Songs. The last scene of their love story talks about her as a little girl, which confuses the Western mind. The point is quite simple and incredibly significant. The growing field of brain science keeps concluding that events in our childhood, whether good or bad, create for us a view of reality and trigger neural pathways in the brain that help us interpret and respond to our experiences. For those with trauma, this can include triggers that bring us back to the most painful parts of life and cause us to become emotionally dysregulated and out of sorts. When we are regulated, we have emotions. When we are dysregulated, our emotions have us. Ongoing dysregulation is a problem, and when we make decisions while dysregulated, we almost always make bad decisions. The only way to heal from the past and have a new beginning for our marriage is to go back to the beginning and learn from it, heal from it, and grow through it so we can move on to a new and good future.

Often, people do not want to go back and revisit the most painful parts of their lives. To go backwards seems like the opposite of progress, which is moving forward to a better future. The truth is, the experiences we have growing up, good and bad, are incredibly formative and began patterns of belief and behavior that we carry with us into adulthood. The growing field of brain science has discovered that early in life, we form attachments to people who love us and build neurological pathways that become somewhat unconscious response patterns that continue throughout life. If those patterns are healthy, such as quickly forgiving those who wrong us and spending time in prayer to unburden, we become healthier, holier, and happier as we journey throughout life. If those patterns are unhealthy, such as becoming embittered and seeking vengeance toward those who wrong us, then we become burdened, bewildered, and broken as we journey throughout life.

Sometimes, the pain we experience today was caused by pain we experienced in the past and did not respond to well. This fact is especially true of trauma. When traumatic events happen, we become emotionally dysregulated. We are not our normal selves, and the trauma causes us to become emotionally out of sorts. This response to trauma is common, and the key is to return to a regulated emotional state with the help of the Holy Spirit as soon as possible. Again, when we are regulated, we have emotions. When we are dysregulated, our emotions have us. We often make our worst decisions and reactions when we are dysregulated, and we form response patterns that are often not good for our long-term well-being.

For example, early in our ministry we met with a couple in which the husband had a good career that generated a lot of income. He really wanted his wife to quit her job so they could have more time together and she could spend more time with their children. She said she wanted the same thing, but she never would quit her job. He tried to be patient, but after a few years of her still working at what was not a high-income job. It caused her a lot of stress, so we met with them. He was stunned when she said, "Growing up, my mom did not have a job, so when my dad ran off with another woman, she became a very poor single mother. She made me promise that I would always have my own income so I could take care of myself." Hearing this, the husband, who adored his wife, burst into tears.

On another occasion, we were meeting with a couple who was having sex only a few times a year, and the wife was genuinely concerned as her young husband showed little interest in intimacy. He said, "Growing up, my mom used sex to manipulate and control my dad. To get sex, he would have to earn it by doing something for my mom, and in return she would sleep with him. Their sex life was more like prostitution, as he would do chores or buy things for her in exchange for sex. Seeing that growing up, I decided that my wife would not use sex to control me, and so if we don't have sex she cannot be in control." Hearing this, the wife, who adored her husband, burst into tears.

Looking back at our childhood and developmental years can help explain who we are, how we think, what we feel, and the decisions we make in the present for good or bad. Many people only want to go forward, but they do not want to go backward to learn from their past. The truth is, sometimes we need to go backward before we can go forward. If you think of it like a bow and arrow, when the string pulls the arrow back, the entire purpose is to prepare it to launch forward with the greatest strength. Just as you could never fire an arrow forward without pulling it backward, sometimes you cannot launch your life forward without going backward to examine your past. This situation is precisely what is happening in the final scene of Song of Songs. We would encourage you to do the same and reflect back. We previously explained how Grace's trauma of assault prior to our meeting surfaced after we had been married over a decade. We had to go back and deal with that evil, heal from it, and forgive it so we could have a new beginning and launch forward into a better future.

Not everyone who reads this book has a marriage that is in a good place. In fact, the entire reason most people pick up a book like this is because something is broken in their marriage. If you are reading this and thinking that you need a new marriage, then you are probably right. That does not, however, mean you need a new spouse. You can have a new marriage with your same spouse. The experts tell us that if a person divorces and then remarries, their odds of divorce in their second marriage are even higher than they were in their first marriage.[xliv] Why is this true? Because a new spouse does not result in new marriage. If the husband and wife start over with God and establish a new beginning, they can have a new marriage and new future. God would love to help you and your spouse have a new mindset, new love, and new grace to live as new people with a new marriage launched from a new beginning. God wants to help you have a new marriage with the same spouse.

> **GOD WOULD LOVE TO HELP YOU AND YOUR SPOUSE HAVE A NEW MINDSET, NEW LOVE, AND NEW GRACE TO LIVE AS NEW PEOPLE WITH A NEW MARRIAGE LAUNCHED FROM A NEW BEGINNING.**

Back to the Future

How did Abbi become the amazing wife we have gotten to know? Throughout the book she is confident and free, and she lives her life to the fullest without falling into sin or folly. To answer that question, she takes us back to the beginning, and her upbringing as a little girl. In this final scene of their epic love story, she returns to review the years when she matured from a little girl to young woman who blossomed into a woman so incredible that an entire book of the Bible tells her story.

Unlike Solomon, who grew up wealthy and surrounded by vineyards, Abbi grew up poor. She considered her chastity and character to be her only vineyard, given to her by God to cultivate, protect, and nourish. From an early age, she took her relationship with God seriously and intently prepared herself to be a godly woman. She very much looked forward to growing up, falling in love, marrying, moving from her mother's home, and having a family.

Throughout the book, her mother and brothers are mentioned but not her father. His absence speaks loudly, as her ancient story sounds very modern—a poor single mother raising two sons who help to look after their sister. The brothers use a most-helpful analogy to explain the two types of young women—doors and walls. I (Grace) was sadly more of a door, as I explained in my trauma story and struggle with my identity in Christ. I thought I deserved to be treated wrongly by guys, was afraid to say no, and was unfortunately not protected by my dad from bad guys. I basically "opened the door" rather than walling myself off to guys who wanted to use me. After suffering abuse and making my own harmful choices, I was determined to raise my daughters differently. For example, our oldest daughter, Ashley, was taught to be more of a wall regarding boys. Mark did an excellent job of appropriately telling her about godly versus ungodly guys, affirming her identity, telling her she was beautiful, and protecting her from those ungodly guys. As her mom, I explained her physical body, changes she would go through, and emotions she would experience as she grew up. I listened and instructed as she talked about all her relationships, especially with boys. I didn't have any brothers, which made boys even more of a mystery. It was helpful for my daughters to have three brothers because it taught them to relate more naturally and learn how to understand how boys work.

A door is either open or can be opened. The entire point of a door is to permit someone access to a place they could not otherwise be. Young women who are open doors tend to attract a lot of attention from young men, most of whom do not have honorable intentions. Having trouble saying no, keeping healthy boundaries, or protecting themselves, these women tend to get hurt in most every way—physically, emotionally, and spiritually. Young women who are closed doors are not as vulnerable, but if the wrong guy knocks on the door, she might open her heart, life, and even body to welcome him in. The brothers decided that if their sister were a door, they would stand guard to protect and defend her from bad guys intent on doing bad things. Humorously, they say that if she were a door, they would behave like a hurricane was coming to town and nail sheets of plywood over the door to ensure it became a wall. You can see how good brothers were a blessing to Abbi—they helped her learn to relate to men, which helped her prepare to be married later in life.

Thankfully, Abbi was a wall and not a door, by her own admission. A wall is the exact opposite of a door. The entire point of a wall is to ensure that no one has access. Young women who are walls are known by young men not to be gullible, vulnerable, or accessible. Such young women don't really struggle to say no, put a guy in his place, or be without a romantic relationship, because they are secure and value their safety. Reflecting back on her life, she is saying that, because she was a wall, she was spared a lot of brokenness and trauma. Today, very few people would share her story, and most of us have some pains, problems, and perils from our past to heal and walk away from.

The Success Sequence

What Abbi is describing is something that sociologists have described as the "success sequence." The success sequence has proven that people can avoid poverty with a 97% success rate, live better lives, and leave better legacies if they do three things in order:

1. Graduate from high school.
2. Work a full-time job.
3. Marry before having children.[xlv]

Christians know God made our planet, made us male and female, and made marriage for sex and children. God's divine design is perfect, and when we follow it, we generally succeed in the same way that, when we honor the laws of gravity created by God, we improve our lives. To sin against God is how we hurt ourselves, our marriages, our children, and our grandchildren.

Before sin entered the world, there was a success sequence established by God for all marriages:

1. Adam and Eve knew God and walked with God before they met.
2. Adam was working a job that would enable him to provide for his family.
3. Adam and Eve were brought together with God's blessing.
4. Adam and Eve did not live together until they were married.
5. Adam and Eve did not consummate their covenant sexually until after they were married.

6. Adam and Eve did not have a child until after they were married.

Putting a life together is like putting anything together— if you read and follow the directions, the odds are better that it will get built right the first time. When you ignore the directions and do what you want, it rarely works, it's frustrating, and it requires you to go back, undo all your wrongs, read the directions, and do it right the second time.

If you look back on your life, any pain you may be experiencing likely started when you violated the directions of God's success sequence. By going back to repent of your sin, learn from it, heal from it, forgive one another for it, and establish a new beginning, you can launch forward to a better future. We had to do this very thing. As we have confessed, we got it wrong, and God helped us to restart and reset to make it right.

God would gladly give you a new beginning and firm foundation for your marriage if that is what you need. For this to benefit your marriage, three things need to happen:

1. *Accept God's grace* for any sin you have committed or has been committed against you in your past. You need God, and you need God's grace, and like any gift, you need to receive it. Only by dealing with your past and healing from it can you be a healthy person and have a healthy future.

2. *Your spouse needs to accept God's grace* for any sin you have committed or has been committed against you in your past. Your spouse needs God's grace and needs to receive that gift. God's grace is applied through the Holy Spirit and has a supernatural cleansing and healing effect on the totality of a person so that your

spouse can be the best version of themselves and work toward the best future for your life together.

3. *Share God's grace with each other.* The love, mercy, kindness, patience, and healing that the Holy Spirit brings to you must flow through you to your spouse. By receiving God's grace, your relationship with God is strengthened but only when you both share God's grace with one another can your marriage be strengthened.

The greatest threat to the success sequence of God's divine design has always been and will always be, the lure of sexual sin in some form or fashion. If you were chaste going into marriage as Abbi was, then we commend you. You are a minority and a minor miracle in our day. For most of us, we have to go back and revisit our premarital years and see how our sexual sin brought shame and suffering.

"Where is the Line?" vs "When is the Time?"

In the previous section, Abbi closed by advising her single friends, "Do not arouse or awaken love until it so desires" (8:4). This important theme occurs throughout the Song of Songs.[68] One English translation (NLT) says, "Not to awaken love until the time is right." Another (GW) says to "Not awaken love or arouse love before its proper time." When walking with God, it's important to understand both His will and His timing. For our personal, romantic relationship, we got God's will right and His timing wrong. It was God's will for us to marry and have a sexual relationship, but God's timing was

---

68 2:7; 3:5; 8:4, 5

to have a sexual relationship only after we were married. We determined to both live as Christians, stop sleeping together, meet with our pastor for Christian counseling, and eventually get married. God honored us putting things back into His success sequence, and we have been faithful to each other for more than three decades! The sin before our marriage, however, did bring suffering into it.

Often, single people will ask the wrong question: "Where is the sexual line in dating?" Generally, single people are looking to push that line as far as they can and then dance on it vigorously. When that is the case, the heart is in a bad place, which means the hands will not be far behind. Ephesians 5:3 says, "There must not be even a hint of sexual immorality ... because these are improper for God's holy people." The question is not "Where is the line?" but rather "When is the time?" The time is your wedding night when you consummate your marriage covenant. Until then, Christians headed toward marriage can spend time together, love and enjoy one another, but until they are husband and wife, they need to act more like brother and sister. Paul says in 1 Timothy 5:1-2, "Treat ... younger women as sisters, with absolute purity." Failure to follow God's plan creates a lot of pains and problems, as we well know having sinned ourselves.

First, the foundation of marriage is not physical but rather spiritual. Since the model for our covenant relationship with our spouse is our covenant relationship with our God, the only way to be healthy and have a healthy marriage is to be a healthy Christian. The love, forgiveness, compassion, and everything else that our marriage needs comes only from God. This fact explains why couples who sleep together often won't pray and worship together, because the intersection of our souls is even deeper than the intersection of our bodies.

Second, God cannot bless a sinful relationship. He does not bless people, but He does bless a place—under His Word. People who place themselves under God's Word with faith-filled obedience are blessed by Him. Conversely, when we disobey Him, we are walking away from His blessing on our relationship.

Third, a couple ignores and overlooks areas of the relationship that need work if they are sexually involved before marriage. Sex becomes a distraction from significant issues that need attention, and even if those issues are known, they are not dealt with because the relational priorities are out of order and the relationship is unhealthy.

Fourth, the man loses the respect of his future wife if the very thing that is a man's deepest God-designed need is taken out of order. A man cannot lead the relationship in the purposes of God while sleeping with his future wife because he has lost his authority, and she has lost respect for him. This puts in motion a relationship set up for conflict and potential failure.

Fifth, the couple establishes a pattern of guilt, shame, and condemnation every time they are together. The latest brain science on neural pathways reveals that when we are sexually active, we are creating, deepening, and habituating our brain pathway. This pattern is a wonderful thing in a relationship that is obedient to God but an awful thing in a relationship that is disobedient to God. If we condition ourselves to have such things as guilt, shame, or condemnation when having sex while dating, then those feelings and neural pathways do not automatically change once we are married. As Paul says in Romans, our entire mind needs to be transformed, and that takes time and training.

The lie in our culture is that the more sex we have and the more sex we watch other people have, the more we will enjoy sex and have it freely and frequently. This powerful lie is simply untrue. For the Christian, the presence of the Holy Spirit in us convicts us of sin, gives us new desires as part of our new nature, and unless we repent of and heal from past sexual sin, we are doing damage to our future marital intimacy. As we learn about the incredible freedom and frankness in the Song of Songs, the refrain of honoring God's timing is crucial. If you failed like us, then we would encourage you to repent to God and one another and extend God's forgiveness to one another. And if needed, we'd encourage you to get professional Christian counseling to have the kind of marriage and sex life that we are learning about in Song of Songs.

> **THE LIE IN OUR CULTURE IS THAT THE MORE SEX WE HAVE AND THE MORE SEX WE WATCH OTHER PEOPLE HAVE, THE MORE WE WILL ENJOY SEX AND HAVE IT FREELY AND FREQUENTLY.**

According to a respected study conducted by non-Christians, people who waited until marriage:

- rated sexual quality 15 percent higher than people who had premarital sex,
- rated relationship stability as 22 percent higher, and
- rated satisfaction with their relationships 20 percent higher.[xlvi]

Additional sociological research confirms,

The new marriage norm for American men and women is to marry around the age of 30, according to the U.S. Census ... But we also have evidence suggesting that religious Americans are less likely to divorce even as they are more likely to marry younger than 30 ...Today, more than 70% of marriages are preceded by cohabitation ... Increased cohabitation is both cause and consequence of the rise in the age at first marriage. But what most young adults do not know is that cohabiting before marriage, especially with someone besides your future spouse, is also associated with an increased risk of divorce, as a recent Stanford study reports. So, one reason that religious marriages in America may be more stable is that religion reduces young adults' odds of cohabiting prior to marriage, even though it increases their likelihood of marrying at a relatively young age. Yes, very young marriage still has risks (as does very late marriage), but religious upbringings seem to partly compensate for those risks, especially among women marrying in their 20s. Our results also suggest that religion fosters relationship stability by pushing young adults away from cohabitation, which is highly unstable, and towards marriage, which is much more stable.[xlvii]

The Bible is true, and eventually science and the social sciences catch up with it. The research confirms that couples who build deeper intimacy in non-sexual areas and then have sex once they are married enjoy deeper intimacy and sexual satisfaction.

If you have done things God's way, then please continue and do not fall into sin as Solomon did and wreck your relationship with God, your spouse, and your children. If you have not done things God's way, then today is the day to start a new beginning with God to have a better future. It is not too late, and God's grace applied through the Holy Spirit's power accelerates healing and progress supernaturally.

As we have confessed, we were not virgins when we met. One of us was a Christian who was not walking closely with the Lord, the other was a non-Christian, and we started sleeping together before we were married. To use an analogy from Jesus, if we would have built our family on this foundation, it would have washed away because it was sand. Thankfully by going back, God allowed us, with the help of wise counsel, godly pastors, and Christian counselors, to get a new beginning and lay a new foundation that has sustained us and our family for three decades of faithful marriage. We have gone back to deal with our past, welcomed God's grace to heal and restore, and shared God's grace with each other. God has been abundantly faithful to launch us forward into a marriage where we are happy, holy, healthy, and still learning, growing, and maturing every day. The fact that God would allow us to have a marriage ministry is a miracle of His grace, and we hope it is an encouragement for you. We are also happy to report that our married children did honor God's divine design and success sequence and are off to a much better beginning than we had. Our hope and prayer for our family is the same as our hope and prayer for your family—that your future would be better and brighter and that each generation of your family would be more holy, healthy, and happy than the generation before, with God's grace flowing stronger and stronger from generation to generation.

Links in the Family Chain

For years, when we have taught on family legacy, we have used a large chain as an analogy. In every chain, there are first links, strong links, weak links, and broken links. The God of the Bible plans generationally, and we should too. Entire books of the Bible, such as Genesis, are multi-generational case studies in marriage and show how decisions made by one married couple positively and negatively affect future generations.[69] Jesus even says He is the God of "Abraham, Isaac, and Jacob" (Matthew 22:32), which is three generations that married and were links in the family chain.

The first link in the chain is the first generation of believers who live as a married couple by God's divine design in the Bible. The first link in the chain faces a lot of pressure from family, temptation from culture, and opposition from Satan to repeat bad and broken generational sin patterns and curses.

A strong link in the chain are healthy Christian marriages that are not the first generation. For example, both of our parents were married over 50 years and are Christians. We are not the first link in the chain but want to be a strong link and raise our children to have godly, endearing, and enduring marriages to continue the legacy of faith in generations of our family.

A weak link in the chain is a marriage that is struggling, stretched, and at risk of breaking. At some point in every marriage, things feel weak, so this is not abnormal. The problem, however, is when a marriage is weak for an extended period of time. Like a chain that is being pulled with great tension, eventually it will break unless the tension is loosened.

---

69 You can find the teaching on Genesis, including sermons in audio and video, sermon notes, sermon transcripts, and study guides, for free at RealFaith.com.

A broken link in the chain is a marriage that has broken and ended. Often, the breaking came in a moment, but it was a weak chain marriage for a prolonged period of time, and eventually it snapped under the pressured tension.

What kind of family did you grow up in?

What kind of marriage do you have today?

What kind of marriage do you want for your future?

If you have children, what kind of marriage do you want to model for future generations?

Our marriage is much bigger than just two people—it is a witness to the world about the difference our God makes and a classroom that is always in session, instructing our children and grandchildren about our God.

Christians talk a lot about receiving God's grace through faith in Jesus Christ so that you can go to heaven when you die, which is true. However, eternal life does not begin the day you die but rather the day you meet Jesus Christ, get a new beginning, and become a new person by His grace. Christianity is not only about dying and going to heaven but also first living a new life with heaven coming to you through the person, presence, and power of the Holy Spirit.

We believe in God, and we believe in marriage. We are certain that the couple who obeys God's divine design for marriage has a 100 percent guarantee of success. God wants His people to live in married love, raise children in homes saturated with grace, and experience generations of blessing! The God who made you and made marriage is for you and always there for you. The same Holy Spirit who raised Jesus Christ from the dead lives in you if you are a Christian, and nothing is too hard for Him.

The best is yet to come!

FACE-TO-FACE QUESTIONS
for Couple Discussion

1. Spend a few hours in private taking turns sharing the story of your upbringing and the good and bad things that helped shape you. Allow your spouse to ask clarifying questions to get to know you at a deeper level.

2. Are there any ways you violated the divine design of God's success sequence that you need a new beginning for?

3. Is there anything from your past that needs to be healed and moved on from because it has set in motion some negative consequences in how you think, feel, and respond when triggered? Is there wise counsel or a Christian professional who can help with this healing process?

4. Is your marriage a first link, strong link, weak link, or broken link today? What do you want it to be in the future and what will you need to do to make that happen?

MAKING YOUR (SEX) MENU!

Every delicacy, both new and old, that I have stored up for you, my beloved.

—Song of Songs 7:13

Often, a good date with our spouse includes a romantic dinner out. As we sit at the table, the person waiting on us lets us know what is on the menu so we can each choose what sounds most desirable for us to enjoy.

Using that same analogy, the wife in the Song of Songs lets her husband know that there is a sexual menu for their marriage. This "homework" assignment should be your favorite part of the book, as we are encouraging you to make your own sexual menu for your marriage.

As we have learned in Song of Songs, they use creative language, and you can do the same. When it comes to our sexual marriage menu, it is good to avoid language that is clinical or crass. Clinical language is used at the doctor's office, and crass language is used in the locker room. Creative language includes the flirtatious, coy, and seductive terms a married couple has as their own private language for their private life.

Appetizers

Appetizers are foreplay. They are fun, tasty things we enjoy before the main course. List all the fun activities that prepare you for the main course as "appetizers" you would like to see on your sexual marriage menu. This shows that you care about the whole person and not just sex itself, as you are willing to wait for the main course.

Main Course

The main courses are the sexual positions and orgasms. The main course is the "protein" part of a meal and the highlight of the sexual marriage menu. This is engaging in full intimacy and enjoyment.

Favorites

Favorites are appetizers and main courses that have remained popular for years. On a restaurant menu, these items are usually featured as perennial favorites—what the restaurant is known for—and the same is true for the sexual marriage menu. Year after year, the couple happily keeps enjoying these favorites.

Off-Menu Specials

Off-menu specials are sexual experiments of new appetizers and main courses that we are not sure we'll like because we've never tried them. In most restaurants, the "chef's special" is a new or seasonal dish that is added to the menu for a short trial to see if it is enjoyable and popular enough to add to the regular menu. For couples who want to explore and experiment without committing to a sexual act they are unfamiliar with, this is considered an off-menu special. As an aside, these can be fun additions to romantic getaways, vacations, and holidays as special treats that might even make it onto the menu.

Dessert

Desserts are the fun things you enjoy after lovemaking such as snuggling, a massage, or additional creative orgasms for the wife. These things are the sweet finish to your time together.

———

Your final assignment is to put together your sexual marriage menu. Some couples have actually printed their sexual menu out and laminated it just like an actual restaurant menu for fun. Too often, our marriage and sex life fall into a predictable routine that is not bad but becomes boring. Chances are, if you spend some time thinking about and looking into your sexual freedoms, your menu will quickly expand, and like the rest of your marriage, it will keep maturing and growing year after year.

   Bon Appetit!

MARK & GRACE DRISCOLL & REALFAITH

Pastor Mark and Grace Driscoll have been married and doing vocational ministry together since 1993. With their five kids, they planted Trinity Church in Scottsdale, Arizona as a family ministry. They are honored and excited to be celebrating 30 years of faithful marriage just before this book releases.

Mark, Grace, and their oldest daughter, Ashley, also started RealFaith Ministries, which contains a mountain of Bible teaching for men, women, couples, parents, pastors, leaders, Spanish speakers, and more. You can access this teaching by visiting **RealFaith.com** or downloading the **RealFaith app.**

Together, Mark and Grace have co-authored *Win Your War* and *Real Marriage,* and he co-authored a father-daughter project called *Pray Like Jesus* with his daughter, Ashley. Pastor Mark has also written numerous other books including *Spirit-Filled Jesus, Who Do You Think You Are?, Vintage Jesus,* and *Doctrine.*

If you have any prayer requests for us, questions for future Ask Pastor Mark or Dear Grace videos, or a testimony regarding how God has used this and other resources to help you learn God's Word, we would love to hear from you at hello@realfaith.com.

Endnotes

i "Modern Marriage," Pew Research Center's Social & Demographic Trends Project (Pew Research Center, July 18, 2007), https://www.pewresearch.org/social-trends/2007/07/18/modern-marriage/.

ii Elizabeth Kuster, "Why Sexless Marriages Happen—And How to Keep It From Happening to You," Prevention, August 6, 2018, https://www.prevention.com/sex/a20499226/the-cure-for-your-sexless-marriage/#.

iii Rachel Scheinerman, "Why Jews Read the Song of Songs on Passover," My Jewish Learning, April 1, 2022, https://www.myjewishlearning.com/article/why-jews-read-the-song-of-songs-on-passover/.

iv William OFlaherty, "Profile of the Screwtape Letters (80th Anniversary)," Essential C.S. Lewis, February 10, 2022, https://essentialcslewis.com/2022/02/10/profile-of-the-screwtape-letters-80th-anniversary/.

v Arend Remmers, "Song of Songs (Song of Solomon)," accessed September 8, 2022, https://biblecentre.org/content.php?mode=7&item=139.

vi Walter A. Elwell and Philip Wesley Comfort, *Tyndale Bible Dictionary*, Tyndale Reference Library (Wheaton, IL: Tyndale House Publishers, 2001), 1198.

vii John D. Barry et al., eds., "Abishag the Shunammite," *The Lexham Bible Dictionary* (Bellingham, WA: Lexham Press, 2016).

viii Sally Lloyd-Jones, *The Jesus Storybook Bible: Every Story Whispers His Name* (Grand Rapids, MI: Zonderkidz, 2009), 36.

ix Jonathan Warren P. (Pagán), "Marriage," in *Lexham Survey of Theology*, ed. Mark Ward et al. (Bellingham, WA: Lexham Press, 2018).

x For examples, see Ken Monday, "There Are 7 Money Personality Types, Says Psychology Expert-How to Tell Which One You Are (and the Pitfalls of Each)," CNBC, April 28, 2021, https://www.cnbc.com/2021/04/28/7-money-personality-types-and-the-pitfalls-of-each.html; Rachel Cruze, "What Are the 7 Money Tendencies?", Ramsey Solutions (Ramsey Solutions, January 26, 2022), https://www.ramseysolutions.com/budgeting/what-are-money-tendencies.

xi Joseph C. Dillow, *Solomon on Sex* (Nashville, TN: Thomas Nelson Publishers, 1973).

xii Robert W. Jenson, *Song of Songs: Interpretation: A Bible Commentary for Teaching and Preaching*, ed. James L. Mays et al. (Louisville, KY: John Knox Press, 2005), 30.

xiii Janet Yuen-Ha Wong et al., "A Comparison of Intimate Partner Violence and Associated Physical Injuries between Cohabitating and Married Women: A 5-Year Medical Chart Review," *BMC Public Health* 16, no. 1 (2016), https://doi.org/10.1186/s12889-016-3879-y.

xiv Glenn T, Stanton, "Cohabitation and Divorce—There Is a Correlation," (Crosswalk.com, October 11, 2011), https://www.crosswalk.com/family/marriage/divorce-and-remarriage/cohabitation-and-divorce-there-is-acorrelation.html#:~:text=Their%20data%20indicates%20that%20people%20with%20cohabiting%20experience,couples%20who%20never%20cohabited.%20A%20Canadian%20sociologist%20explains%3A.

xv For more information, see Roni Beth Tower, "3 Family Styles: Which Best Describes Yours?", *Psychology Today* (Sussex Publishers), accessed September 10, 2022, https://www.psychologytoday.com/us/blog/life-refracted/201806/3-family-styles-which-best-describes-yours.

xvi John Gottman and Nan Silver, *The Seven Principles for Making Marriage Work* (New York: Three Rivers Press, 1999), 2.

xvii Gottman and Silver, 32.

xviii Ibid, 32–39.

xix John D. Barry et al., *Faithlife Study Bible* (Bellingham, WA: Lexham Press, 2012, 2016), So 4:16.

xx John A. Balchin, "The Song of Songs," in *New Bible Commentary: 21st Century Edition*, ed. D. A. Carson et al., 4th ed. (Leicester, England; Downers Grove, IL: Inter-Varsity Press, 1994), 623.

xxi Elwell and Comfort, *Tyndale Bible Dictionary*, 895.

xxii "32 Shocking Divorce Statistics," McKinley Irvin Family Law, November 7, 2019, https://www.mckinleyirvin.com/family-law-blog/2012/october/32-shocking-divorce-statistics/.

xxiii Gottman and Silver, 19.

xxiv Ibid, 19–20.

xxv "Social Capital vs. Financial Capital," Done by Forty, September 22, 2014, https://www.donebyforty.com/2014/09/social-capital-vs-financial-capital.html.

xxvi Kimberly Holland, "Phubbing: What Is It, Effects on Relationships, and How to Stop" (Healthline Media, June 5, 2018), https://www.healthline.com/health/phubbing.

xxvii Gabriella Paiella, "Man Marries Phone to Make a Statement about Society, but It's Actually A Pretty Good Idea" (The Cut, June 28, 2016), https://www.thecut.com/2016/06/man-marries-phone-las-vegas.html.

xxviii Katie Golem, "How Your Smartphone Might Sabotage Your Relationship," The Gottman Institute, February 10, 2021, https://www.gottman.com/blog/smartphone-might-sabotage-relationship/.

xxix "Brain Anatomy and How the Brain Works," Johns Hopkins Medicine, July 14, 2021, https://www.hopkinsmedicine.org/health/conditions-and-diseases/anatomy-of-the-brain.

xxx Julie Beck, "Roman Plumbing: Overrated," The Atlantic (Atlantic Media Company, November 13, 2019), https://www.theatlantic.com/health/archive/2016/01/ancient-roman-toilets-gross/423072/.

xxxi Duane A. Garrett, *Proverbs, Ecclesiastes, Song of Songs*, vol. 14, The New American Commentary (Nashville: Broadman & Holman Publishers, 1993), 420.

xxxii Garret, *Proverbs, Ecclesiastes, Song of Songs*, 421.

xxxiii Othmar Keel, *A Continental Commentary: The Song of Songs* (Minneapolis, MN: Fortress Press, 1994), 225.

xxxiv John D. Barry et al., *Faithlife Study Bible*, So 7:2.

xxxv Craig Glickman, "Song of Songs," in *CSB Study Bible: Notes*, ed. Edwin A. Blum and Trevin Wax (Nashville, TN: Holman Bible Publishers, 2017), 1031.

xxxvi John G. Snaith, "The Song of Songs 7:1-5," in *The New Century Bible Commentary: The Song of Songs*, (Grand Rapids, MI: Marshall Pickering and Wm. B. Eerdmans, 1993), 101.

xxxvii Joseph Dillow et al., *Intimacy Ignited: Discover the Fun and Freedom of God-Centered Sex* (Colorado Springs, CO: NavPress, 2014), 209.

xxxviii Craig Glickman, "Song of Songs," 1032.

xxxix Scott Edwards, "Love and the Brain," Harvard Medical School, 2015, https://hms.harvard.edu/news-events/publications-archive/brain/love-brain.

xl Ibid.

xli Luciana Gravotta, "Be Mine Forever: Oxytocin May Help Build Long-Lasting Love," Scientific American, February 12, 2013, https://www.scientificamerican.com/article/be-mine-forever-oxytocin/.

xlii Scott Edwards, "Love and the Brain."

xliii Joseph Dillow et al., *Intimacy Ignited: Discover the Fun and Freedom of God-Centered Sex.*

xliv Brittany Wong, "Second Marriages Are More Likely to End in Divorce. Here's Why," HuffPost, March 3, 2017, https://www.huffpost.com/entry/second-marriages-are-more-likely-to-end-in-divorce-heres-why_n_58b88e38e4b0b99894162a07.

xlv "What Does the Success Sequence Mean?", Institute for Family Studies, February 25, 2021, https://ifstudies.org/blog/what-does-the-success-sequence-mean.

xlvi Bill Hendrick, "Benefits in Delaying Sex until Marriage," (WebMD, December 28, 2010), https://www.webmd.com/sex-relationships/news/20101227/theres-benefits-in-delaying-sex-until-marriage.

xlvii Lyman Stone and W. Bradford Wilcox, "The Religious Marriage Paradox: Younger Marriage, Less Divorce," AEI, December 16, 2021, https://www.aei.org/articles/the-religious-marriage-paradox-younger-marriage-less-divorce/.

NOTES

NOTES

NOTES